First published in the United States of America in 2021 by
GalaTag Ltd.
9115 Knightsland Trail, Houston, Texas 77083. Tel 832-856-5152

The rights of Rose Mbamali to be identified as the author of this publication.
All rights reserved. No part of this book may be reproduced, stored in a retrieval system,
or transmitted, in any form or by any means, electronic, mechanical, photocopying,
recording, or otherwise without the prior written permission of the copyright holders.

ISBN: 978-0-578-90699-7

PREPARATION FOR OUR JOURNEY TO HEAVEN

TABLE OF CONTENTS

i   Dedication
ii   Attestations
iii   Foreword
iv   Preface

Chapter 1 Salvation, the first work of grace.	18
Chapter 2 Assurance of Salvation.	23
Chapter 3 Quiet Time.	29
Chapter 4 What is Prayer?	36
Chapter 5 Water Baptism.	40
Chapter 6 Sanctification, the second work of grace.	44
Chapter 7 The Holy Spirit: A divine personality.	54
Chapter 8 The Holy Spirit Baptism.	61
Chapter 9 Spread the Word.	67
Chapter 10 Forgiveness is important for our heavenly journey.	72
Chapter 11 Give God His rightful place.	78
Chapter 12 Charitable deeds, prayer and fasting.	84
Chapter 13 The Lord's Supper.	90
Chapter 14 The Rapture and the Great Tribulation.	94
Chapter 15 The Millennium, Resurrections and Judgments.	103
Chapter 16 Backsliding, a serious hindrance.	108
Chapter 17 Intercessors needed.	114
Chapter 18 Home at last: Heaven or Hell?	121
Chapter 19 What a friend we have in Jesus.	130

DEDICATION

This book is dedicated to the Father, Son and the Holy Spirit who called me to minister through the written word. God has given me the strength and grace to complete this book in good health. The book is also dedicated to:

All the members of Fountain of Living Waters Ministry, your love, enthusiasm, and support helped me to teach you with joy. The Leaders who were always there for me and the prayer warriors who kept the fire burning.

My children, sons and daughters in law, grandchildren, and great grandchild. You are my joy and the thought of you lengthens my days.

My only surviving sibling, Theresa Osuma who labors day and night for me in prayer.

ATTESTATION

I consider it a privilege and an honor, for the opportunity to introduce Mrs. Rose Mbamali. In this capstone of her ministry work: "Preparation for our journey to heaven" her training and experiences, as an educator, a mentor and a leader, a diligent effort has been made to narrate the process of salvation by grace through faith, growing in the knowledge of our Lord Jesus, and steadfastness in our walk, as disciples to the end.

This is a must read for anyone, who may be seeking for meaning and truth in life, and those that need affirmation, of the gospel's efficacy.

Pastor Charles Ochei
African Missionary Foundation,
Houston, Texas.

I am honored and excited for this opportunity to introduce Mrs. Rose Mbamali, whom I fondly call 'mummy'. She is an amazing woman of God, teacher, disciple of Christ, and mother to many. Her passion, steadfastness and tenacity to share the gospel are admirable and beyond comprehension. Mrs. Mbamali is one of the most inspiring persons I have come across. Her dedication to spreading the good news is revealed in her life style and now in her book, 'Preparation for Our Journey to Heaven', a reflection of her articulate style of leadership, mentoring, and nurture. This book offers a step by step guide to salvation and how to uphold a daily walk with Christ afterward. Mrs. Mbamali shares her wealth of experience and wisdom as she educates us on the importance of sustaining our salvation through reverence and continued fellowship with God, forgiveness, and living for eternity.

I know you will be blessed by this book, so I encourage you to share it with others and spread the good news. Enjoy!

Dr. Owen Therese Imachukwu
Georgia, USA

This book is made to assist you to discover what God has said concerning the time of the end and the calamities that will come after.

Today many people are no longer committed to follow up with the events through the end time prophecies according to the Bible. These prophecies are gradually losing their importance in the minds of people, even though the fulfillment of the prophecies is often overlooked.

Minister Rose Mbamali has written to highlight us about the dangers of ignoring the word and the warning of the Lord concerning the timing of the end time. The 19 chapters of this book is highly recommended, it is highly informative directing us back to God as the coming of the Lord is closing up. I sincerely recommend this book to you personally as a tool to preparing you to meet the Lord Jesus Christ and to spend eternity with Him.

This book is a clear revelation of God to bring you back to God's principles. A loaded package to prepare you to be safe from the coming disasters. The book will help you to come back to your senses for a total repentance because God's standard remains sure. Take a decision today so that you will not be left behind. Place your faith in Christ Jesus for God's true desire was clearly demonstrated when He sent His one and only Son Jesus Christ to die for you so you will be saved. Enjoy the ride and be rapturable.

Your friend and Pastor
Obi Edward Onyekachukwu
International Co-ordinator
Caresforlife International Gospels Foundation.
A missionary outreach.
P. O. Box 1701. Voorhees
New Jersey USA.

FOREWORD

I was overawed when I was invited to write the Foreword of the marvelous piece by Mrs. Rose Mbamali titled 'Preparation for our journey to heaven' because I felt the least worthy of that privilege. But then, I remembered that Apostle Paul was perhaps the least qualified of the Apostles and yet he did great wonders in the name of our Lord Jesus Christ. Mrs. Mbamali has (for over two decades that I have known her as my mother-in-law, mother and prayer warrior) been consistent in her journey to heaven and readily shed every stumbling block (vestiges of sin) to this great journey. I always marveled at her tenacity of purpose and the doggedness with which she approached issues pertaining to the 'Way' who we all know is Jesus Christ, the Author and finisher of our faith.

Mrs. Mbamali from early times made it clear that her joy would not be complete if she did not ensure that as many sisters and brothers who hearken to the voice of God would make the journey to heaven. And so, she started the evangelism journey despite her privileged position which she shed along the way, preferring humility to arrogance, practically washing the feet of all she encountered on her journey. This book has been long in coming and a welcome guide for all who genuinely desire a place at our father's table when the earthly mission is complete. Indeed, in John 14:2 Christ assured His Disciples thus: 'My father's house has many rooms, I am going there to prepare a place for you'.

In Chapter 1 of this exciting, soul searching and riveting work, the author discusses Salvation as the first work of grace. In her view, of all the questions confronting humans, the most important deserving prompt attention should be: 'What happens after we die'?

'Where do we spend eternity?' Through Psalm 15 and a consideration of such biblical matters as who Jesus is and why we need him, the author provides answers to these pertinent and life defining questions. The highlight of the second Chapter is the assurance of salvation which is the hope of every Christian and how sin is an obstacle to the actualization of that hope. There is also a discussion of how to live without sin, the fulcrum of which is to practice being in the presence of God.

In Chapter three, the author discusses 'quiet time' which is a fundamental principle of all those who want to commune with our Heavenly Father on an individual basis with no distractions or any form of disturbance. Indeed, the author rightly points out that quiet time is one of the ways a Christian acquires spiritual strength and growth. Guidance is provided on how to have a quiet time and some prayer points for family devotion. Perhaps the most powerful exposition of one of the major steps of the journey to heaven is the discussion on prayer in Chapter 4 and the dissection of the model prayer 'Our Father' which Jesus taught His disciples. The author makes it clear in no uncertain terms that praying in the name of Jesus makes the kingdom of darkness quake and works many miracles for believers.

The importance of Water Baptism is discussed in Chapter 5 as the next step after Salvation through repentance and faith in Christ. The author describes Baptism (and rightly so) as an important foundation for the Christian life. She concludes by cautioning that water baptism is mandatory, not optional as a public declaration of discipleship of Christ. She warns that if we deny Him, He will deny us before His Father.

In Chapter 6, the author focuses on sanctification as the second work of Grace.

The true meaning of Sanctification was discussed with clarity while some erroneous doctrines concerning the subject were highlighted. Having elucidated on the many benefits of sanctification, Mrs. Mbamali concludes the chapter with an exhortation of God: 'Be ye holy for I am holy'. She noted that sanctification is by the grace of God. The divine personality of the Holy Spirit was discussed in Chapter 7 with an explanation of the symbols, the work and various relationships of the Holy Spirit. The author warns of the consequences of blaspheming against the Holy Spirit and admonishes all to reject any prophesy or teaching that is not according to God's word.

In Chapter 8, the author elaborated on the Holy Spirit Baptism, its benefits and the universality of the Holy Spirit Baptism. In the author's words, "The Holy Spirit Baptism is for all who meet God's conditions." The author in Chapter 9 invites all to harken to the call of evangelism by spreading the good news. She explained the 'Romans road' to evangelism and notes that just as there is a reward for winning souls, there is judgment for not warning sinners.

One of the most difficult injunctions of God in the eyes of men is forgiveness. The author in Chapter 10 emphasizes the importance of forgiveness for our heavenly journey. She draws on the model prayer, (Our Lord's prayer) to illustrate the reciprocal nature of our forgiving others as a basis for God's forgiveness of our own sins.

In Chapter 11, the reader is admonished to give God His rightful place and not incur God's anger by giving His place to God's own creatures, otherwise known as idolatry.
The author informs the reader in Chapter 12 that charitable deeds, prayer and fasting are essential for the journey to heaven.

Using biblical verses, the reader is invited to note the deeds that get heaven's attention and what the Bible teaches about fasting. The significance of the Lord's Supper is discussed in Chapter 13, particularly the declaration of Christ that we should 'Do this in remembrance of Me'. The conditions for receiving the Lord's Supper were enumerated and the author notes that the Lord's Supper is a family meal that binds us to the love and care of one another even as we look forward to His coming.

Chapter 14 discusses the rapture, the great tribulation and the signs of the coming of the Lord. The tribulation arising from the failure of the world to believe in Jesus Christ who paid the price for our sins was brought to the consciousness of the reader by the author using a lot of imagery from Bible verses on the subject. Also using a lot of imagery, the author in Chapter 15 discusses the millennium, resurrections and judgments. She notes that though God is the God of love, He must deal with sin in His judgment throne and with sinners too.

Backsliding as a stumbling block in the race to heaven is the focus of Chapter 16. The signs of backsliding which believers should guard against were copiously enumerated and a guide for returning to God is provided for those who may have fallen victim of the dangerous bug of backsliding. Chapter 17 highlights the need for intercessors.

The defining point of our existence is when we have to, at our journey's end, reckon with the question: Heaven or Hell? Where will be home at the end of our earthly journey? Those are the questions the author seeks to answer in Chapter 18. In her characteristic candor, Mrs. Mbamali explains that Heaven is where God Himself will dwell with His children forever while Hell is where the devil and his angels will spend eternity. The friendship of Jesus which is the central theme of this work and the life of every believer is evaluated in the concluding Chapter 19. The abiding love of Jesus for all, including sinners, despite His hatred of sin is made manifest in the words of Jesus Himself 'Do not fear little flock, for it is your Father's good pleasure to give you the Kingdom' Luke 12:32.

The author reminds us of the promise of Jesus to give us abundant life if only we will make Him our best friend. Is anything stopping you from making Jesus your best friend? Have you accepted Him as your Lord and Savior? As for me and my household, we will only serve the Lord in our journey to Heaven.

I wish to use this opportunity to invite all whose lives have been touched in one way or another by the enduring work Mrs. Mbamali has been doing in the Lord's vineyard to purchase copies of this book and to also make it available to the ends of the earth. The book will serve as an invaluable resource for theologians, Ministers of the Word, believers and unbelievers alike as well as all those craving a genuine reconciliation with God.

I pray that all who read this book will be renewed with vigor for the journey to heaven so that our Father's house will be filled to the brim. That is what I believe the author set out to achieve through the painstaking research and well written Chapters of this book. May the author's vision in this regard be accomplished in Jesus name. Amen.

Anthony I. Ibekwe Esq.
Partner, Opal Law Office,
Lagos, Nigeria.

PREFACE

I founded the "Fountain of Living Waters Ministry," a teleconference Bible study and Prayer Ministry in October 2012. The Ministry is a non-denominational assembly of the followers of Christ. My desire for this ministry is that the unadulterated word of God is taught in a consistent manner now and after I have gone to be with the Lord. This led me to start the process of handing over the work I had started to the younger members of the Ministry in 2015, when I turned 75 years old. In July 2019, the Lord laid it on my heart to write my messages in a book; It then dawned on me that writing the messages in a book will be another way of handing over the Ministry to the younger members. I never thought of writing a book, but it was clear to me that the Lord in laying it on my heart to do so, had said the word "Journey." Having meditated on this, I wrote down the word. I am happy that God approved my teaching which I know was guided by the Holy Spirit.

As I pondered more on why the Lord had said the word "Journey," I remembered that the focus of my teaching in the Ministry has been on how to know and do the will of God, so that we can have eternal life in heaven. The transition from earth to heaven or hell is like a journey. You need to prepare as travelers do, so I titled the book 'Preparation for Our Journey to Heaven.' There are a few things the Lord requires of us in order to be with Him in Heaven. First is to be reconciled with Him. Matt. 6: 33 says, "Seek first the Kingdom of God and its righteousness and other things will be added to you." (John 1:12, 3:3-8; Acts 17:30-31) He also wants us to be Holy because He is Holy. (Micah 6:8; Hebrews 12:14;1 Peter 1:16). God has provided all that we need, to meet these goals. Jesus paid the price on the cross and His grace is always available and sufficient.

Since making Heaven involves reading, believing and doing the word of God, this book is more of a Bible study guide. The Bible is the book that binds us together. God's word changes lives. (John 15:3; 2 Timothy 3:16; Hebrews 4:12). In our Ministry, we teach the word verse by verse, from Genesis to Revelation. This expository method of teaching the word has always yielded good fruit. The Holy Spirit has helped us emulate the life of the New Testament Church. The love of the brethren is vivid; giving to the needy is from the heart, asking for forgiveness is done according to the word of God. Many lives are being changed and God's work is done to please Him and not the leaders of the Ministry. I strongly believe in Biblical Christianity and that this book, will open your spiritual eyes to the things of God and truly prepare you for heaven. If the messages by our Prayer Ministry, has affected lives positively, and made our members better Christians, then reading and learning from this book will surely take you to a higher spiritual level.

The topics discussed in the various chapters will teach you the different things you should do or avoid in order to reach the finish line, and places emphasis on the fact that you have the free will to either obey God's commandment and spend eternity in heaven or disobey His commandment and spend eternity with Satan in hell.

I am indebted to my pastor and mentor W.F. Kumuyi (General Superintendent of Deeper Christian Life Ministry) under whose anointing I gave my life to Christ. He is a "holiness preacher" who lives by the word he preaches. I was privileged to have served in some leadership roles for fifteen years in Deeper Christian Life Ministry before I left Nigeria for the United States of America.
In my Christian walk, I pray to be like Prophet Samuel and Apostle Paul, who taught their followers all they knew and gave all for the

Kingdom work. "Moreover, as for me, God forbid that I should sin against the Lord in ceasing to pray for you: but I will teach you the good and the right way." (1Samuel 12:23). I wrote this book to teach those who are willing to learn all that the Lord has taught me concerning what we need to do to make heaven. Paul says in 1Corintians 11:1, "Be ye followers of me, even as I also am of Christ." Let us be careful who we follow and emulate. Let our eyes be focused on Jesus and on Jesus alone.

The knowledge I acquired from Deeper Christian Life Ministry was a great resource in writing this book. Some of my writings and ideas were taken from the book "Life in the Spirit Study Bible" by Donald Stamp and John Wesley, and its subsequent translation into the Igbo language by the same authors, are a treasure to our Ministry. Some other helpful resources were from 'Amplified Study Bible,' by The Lockman Foundation; 'Jeremiah Study Bible,' by Dr. David Jeremiah and 'The Bible exposition commentary' by Warren W. Wiersbe. Important ideas also came from messages by Pastors T. O. Banso and Gbile Akanni. I am thankful to these men of God whose hard work enabled me to write this book with confidence.

I want to express my sincere gratitude to my children Ngozi Ozoh, Emeka Mbamali, Ifeanyi Mbamali and Chinazor Ibekwe for their tremendous support and encouragement throughout this journey. Very special thanks to my son in law, Anthony Ibekwe who gave so much of his time, proofread, edited the entire manuscript and also wrote a brilliant foreword. This acknowledgement will not be complete without giving heartfelt thanks to Zika Ozoh my granddaughter who edited large portions of the manuscript and ran errands when necessary to assist me in accomplishing this goal.

The purpose of writing this book will be accomplished if as many people as possible read it and take the time to ask and answer the question, "Where will I spend eternity?"
This book should be a Bible study guide in every home and a must have for your loved ones who I believe, will want to experience the joy of heaven at last.

I pray that as you read this book, you will determine to walk in the Spirit and not in the flesh, that you will live a consistent life of prayer and holiness, pursue peace with all men, remember the needy, trust God and hold fast to your profession of faith and have compassion for lost souls. In a nutshell, I urge you to have the mind of Christ and live with eternity in view.

Minister Rose N. Mbamali
Fountain of Living Waters Ministry
Virginia, USA

CHAPTER 1

SALVATION, THE FIRST WORK OF GRACE

We always have questions about our environment, or future, our plans and aspirations. I believe that the most important question we should ask is "what happens after we die?" Or "Where do we spend eternity? King David sought to know who would be qualified to live with God in Heaven.

The answer can be found in Psalm 15 as follows:

PSALM 15
1 O Lord, who may lodge (as a guest) in your tent?
Who may dwell (continually) on Your holy hill?
2 He who walks with integrity and
strength of character and works righteousness,
And speaks and holds truth in his heart.
3 He does not slander with his tongue,
Nor does evil to his neighbor
Nor takes up a reproach against his friend;
4 In his eyes an evil person is despised
But he honors those who fear the Lord
(and obediently worship Him with awe-inspired
reverence and submissive wonder)
He keeps his word even to his own disadvantage and does not change it. (for his own benefit);
5 He does not put out his money at
Interest (to a fellow Israelite)
And does not take a bribe against the innocent.
He who does these things will never be shaken.
(Amplified Study Bible)

God is holy. Man is sinful and needs to be regenerated. Jesus, the Son of God is the only one who is qualified to dwell in God's holy hill because He is without sin. Jesus is holy. God's eyes are too pure to behold evil so He sent His only son to save us from sin and show us the way to Heaven. Jesus declared in John 14: 6 "I am the way, the truth and the life; No man cometh unto the father but by me." In John 10:9 Jesus says, "I am the door: by me if any man enters in, he shall be saved, and shall go in and out, and find pasture." (King James version) If Jesus is the Way and the Door to Heaven, how can we find Him?

Who is Jesus?
Many people, even non- Christians have heard the story of Jesus. But who is Jesus? Jesus is Christ, the anointed one. He is the son of God. He was both God and Man; two individuals united in one personality. "As man, He was thirsty; as God, He gave living water. As man, He went to a wedding; as God, He turned water to wine. As man, He slept in a boat; as God, He stilled the storm. As man, He was tempted; as God, He sinned not; As man, He wept; as God, He raised Lazarus from the dead. As man, He prayed; as God, He makes intercession for all men." Apostle Paul summaries this in 1Timothy 3:16 "And great, we confess, is the mystery (the hidden truth) of godliness: He (Jesus Christ) who was revealed in human flesh, was justified and vindicated in the Spirit, seen by angels, preached among the nations, believed on in the world, taken up to glory." (Amplified Study Bible). Jesus is the Prince of Peace. He is our Redeemer. He redeemed us from the slave market of sin and sickness. He is the Living Word. John 1:14. He is the Light of the world; John 1:7–9. He is our Mediator; 1 Timothy 2:5. He is the Judge of the world; John 5:27. He is the Resurrection and life; John 11: 25. He is our intercessor; Hebrews 7:25. Jesus is our Savior, Baptizer, Healer, and coming King.

He is the King of kings and Lord of lords. He is the Captain of our salvation. He is our Perfect Sacrifice. He is our Helper in time of need. At the mention of the name of Jesus every knee in Heaven, earth and under the sea will bow. This book definitely cannot contain all that Jesus is. Jesus is the theme of the Bible from Genesis to Revelation. "What the hub is to the wheel, Jesus Christ is to the Bible."

Why we need Jesus.
In the Old Testament, the blood of animals was used as atonement for sins. God accepted that sacrifice for it is the blood that makes atonement. Leviticus 17:11. In the book of Hebrews, the 9th chapter verse 22 says "that without the shedding of the blood, there is no forgiveness of sin." Jesus fulfilled the conditions laid down by God for our sins to be forgiven when He shed His blood on the cross of Calvary. Jesus, the son of God came down to earth in the form of man to reconcile man with God. He shed His blood, from the whipping, when the crown of thorns pierced His brow and when the nails pierced His hands and feet. Man was warned that curses would follow if he does not keep God's commandment. (Deuteronomy 28:15 -68). Man disobeyed God and so was cursed. A cursed man is punished by hanging on a tree. Jesus was crucified on the tree to pay the price for our sins and bear the punishment for our curses. (Galatians 3:13). "Christ has redeemed us from the curse of the law, having become a curse for us for it is written "Cursed is everyone who hangs on a tree." (NKJV). Jesus is our Perfect Sacrifice.

We need Jesus to be our Lord and Savior because He died for our sins and He is the Judge that will judge all mankind. "For as the Father hath life in himself; so hath he given to the son to have life in himself; and hath given him authority to execute judgment also, because he is the son of man." (John 5:26-27 KJV).

The purpose of Christ's first coming was not to judge the world but to show us the way of salvation. John 3:17-18 reads "For God sent not his son into the world to condemn the world; but that the world through him might be saved. He that believeth on him is not condemned but he that believeth not is condemned already, because he has not believed in the name of the only begotten Son of God." (KJV). You will notice that it is "the name" of the Son of God that we believe in. That 'name' is Jesus. No one has seen God so He gave us the name of His Son. The scripture teaches that the just shall live by faith. It is by faith that you receive Jesus into your life.

HOW TO RECEIVE JESUS AS LORD AND SAVIOR:

Read these scriptures: Romans 3:23, 6:23, 5:8; Proverbs 28:13; Isaiah 55:6 – 7; Romans 10:9, 10, 13; 1 Corinthians 6:9 -10; Ephesians 5: 1- 5.

REPENTANCE: You must acknowledge that you are a sinner. All men have sinned against God. God set a standard which man did not meet. We all came short of the glory of God. You must accept that Jesus was nailed to the cross because of your sins, and be sorry from the depth of your heart that you caused Him such deep agony.

CONFESS YOUR SINS TO GOD: Confess your sins to God by naming those sins one after the other, it does not matter how many times you committed each sin. God knows all of them but He wants you to call them by name so that you don't go back to commit those sins again. If you decide to sincerely turn away from your sins the Holy Spirit will remind you of the sins you have committed. As you confess your sins, ask God to forgive you and give you the grace to forsake them.

God delights in the repentance of a sinner and the Angels rejoice when a sinner repents. We are saved by grace and not by works. (Ephesians 2:8–9).

ASK JESUS TO COME INTO YOUR LIFE AS YOUR LORD AND SAVIOR
Having asked for the forgiveness of your sins, believe that your sins are forgiven and washed away by the blood of Jesus. The blood of Jesus washes away our sins. (1 John 1:7). Pray and thank God for forgiving you and ask Jesus to please come into your heart. The Holy Spirit will now take over and dwell in you. He will guide and direct you. Remember that asking Jesus to be your Lord demands implicit obedience.
(John 1:12, Ephesians 3:17–19, John 8:11, Romans 6:6-10, 12,14).

A PRAYER FOR SALVATION (SAMPLE PRAYER)
My Lord and my God, I know that I am a sinner and my sins have separated me from you. The Bible tells me that you died on the cross because of my sins and the sins of the whole world. You paid this price even while I was still in sin. You rose from the dead that I might have eternal life. I am very sorry that I have made you unhappy. Please Father, forgive me. (Mention the sins you remember).
Please Lord give me the grace not to sin again.
I forsake these sins and with your help Lord, I will live for you. Lord Jesus, please come into my heart and live forever. Thank you, Father for an answered prayer, for in Jesus name, I pray. Amen.

CHAPTER 2

ASSURANCE OF SALVATION

If you have prayed the prayer in the preceding chapter with a sincere heart, believe that God has answered. When God forgives our sins, He puts them in the sea of forgetfulness. He will never remember them again. (Micah 7: 18 -19).
Believe in the promises of God that do not fail and live a new life in Christ as a child of God. Old things are passed away and all things have become new. (2 Cor. 5:17). Genuine repentance will be accompanied by the fruits of righteousness. True saving faith and conversion must become evident through lives that forsake sin and bear godly fruit. God our Father hates sin so every child of God must hate sin. Be as your Father.

SINS OF THE FLESH VERSUS THE FRUIT OF THE SPIRIT:
In Galatians 5:19–23, Apostle Paul lists the sins of the flesh and contrasts them with the single-minded lifestyle called "the fruit of the Spirit." This is a cluster of fruits, though they are nine in number, a believer in Christ bears this fruit as a confirmation of the work of the Holy Spirit in him.

Let me explain a few of the sins of the flesh in Galatians 5 which most people indulge in and may not be aware that they offend God. When you offend God, you are a sinner.
1."**Emulations:** Resentfulness, envy of another's success. Whatever anyone has is given by God. We should not envy such a person. God has a reason for allowing him to succeed.

2. **Wrath:** Explosive anger that flames into violent words or deeds. (Col. 3:8) Only the grace of God can help anyone overcome such anger.

3. **Heresies:** Division within the congregation into exclusive groups or cliques that destroy the unity of the church. (1 Cor. 11:19) If we believe the whole teaching of the Bible, there will be no room for division.

4. **Drunkenness:** Impairing one's mental or physical control by alcoholic drink." (Life in the Spirit Study Bible). You should not take pleasure in anything that will destroy your health. Seeing that some of the things we do and tend to overlook are contrary to God's will for us, we should flee from sin and come to terms with Jesus.

Paul ends the list of the sins of the flesh in Galatians 5:21, with the words, "I warn you beforehand, just as I did previously, that those who practice such things will not inherit the Kingdom of God." What will it profit a man if he gains the whole world and loses his soul? Think about this.

THE FRUIT OF THE SPIRIT: "This is produced in God's children as they allow the Holy Spirit to direct and influence their lives and they walk in fellowship with God. (Romans 8:12–14)

1. **Love:** A caring for and seeking the highest good of another person without motive of personal gain. (Romans 5:5; 1 Corinthians.13:1 - 8; Ephesians 5:2; Colossians 3:14)

2. **Joy:** The feeling of gladness based on the love, grace, blessings, promises and nearness of God that belongs to those who believe in Christ. (Psalm 119:16; 2 Corinthians 6:10; 12:9; 1 Peter 1:8).

3. **Peace:** The rest of heart and mind based on the knowledge that all is well between the believer and his heavenly Father, resulting in freedom from turmoil of anxiety. (Romans 15:33; Philippians 4:7; 1Thes. 5:23; Hebrews 13:20-21).

4. **Long suffering:** Endurance, patience; being slow to anger or despair. (Ephesians 4:2; 2 Timothy 3:10; Hebrews 12:1).

5. **Gentleness:** Kindness; not wanting to hurt anyone or cause them pain. (Ephesians 4:32; Colossians 3:12; 1 Peter 2:3).

6. **Goodness:** Zeal for truth and righteousness and a hatred for evil, it can be expressed in acts of kindness. (Luke 7:37-50) or in rebuking and correcting evil. (Matt. 21:12–13).

7. **Faith:** Firm and unswerving loyalty to a person to whom one is united by promise, commitment, trust, and honesty. (Matt. 23:23; Romans 3:3; 1Timothy 6:12; 2 Timothy 2:2; 4:7; Titus 2:10).

8. **Meekness:** Gentleness; restraint coupled with strength and courage. It describes a person who can be angry when anger is needed and humbly submissive when submission is needed.
(2 Timothy 2:25; 1 Peter 3:15; 2 Corinthians 10:1; Numbers 12:3).

9. **Temperance:** Self- control; mastering one's own desires and passions, including faithfulness to one's marriage vows; and purity (1 Corinthians 7:9; 9:25; Titus 1:8; 2:5).

At the end of Galatians 5:23, Paul writes "against such there is no law." This means that there are no restrictions to the lifestyle of bearing the fruit of the Spirit. Christians must practice these virtues over and over again as there is no law prohibiting them from living according to these principles." (Life in the Spirit Study Bible).

HOW TO LIVE A LIFE WITHOUT SIN:
(Practice being in the presence of God).
1. Believe that God loves you and that He is everywhere. (Psalm 34:15).
2. Nothing is hidden from God, therefore I will not sin, because sin makes God sad and He sees me. (Hebrews 4:13; Psalm 139:7–12)
3. Any time the devil wants you to sin, say "No" to him and remind him that God watches over you in love. Tell him
"I CANNOT OFFEND MY GOD." (Titus 2:11-14). In Genesis 39:9, Joseph asks "How then can I do this great wickedness, and sin against God?"
4. If you sin, immediately repent and confess that sin to God. He always forgives those who are really sorry for their sins (1 John 1:9).
5. A child of God does not continue in sin. (1 John 3:9).
6. We are all called to follow Jesus by faith. Nobody has ever seen God. (1 John 4:12; Romans 1:17).
7. Forgive anyone who offends you because Christ forgave you your sins. The Bible teaches that if we do not forgive others, God will not forgive us. (Ephesians 4:32. Matthew 6:14-15). 1 Corinthians 13:4-7 reads "Love suffers long and is kind; love does not envy; love does not parade itself, is not puffed up; **5** does not behave rudely, does not seek its own, is not provoked, thinks no evil; **6** does not rejoice in iniquity; but rejoices in the truth; **7** bears all things, believes all things, hopes all things, endures all things". (NKJV). He who does not love, does not know God, for God is Love. It is love that helps us forgive others.

In my Christian walk, I have learned that the best way to forgive someone who has offended you, no matter the gravity of the offence, is to pray that God will bless him and help him to know the truth. It is usually tough at the beginning.

Force yourself to say good things about the offender in your prayer. If you continue that spiritual exercise for 3 to 6 months, the Holy Spirit will take over and you will find yourself praying in love and meaning all you say concerning him. Do not revenge or retaliate. Stay on the Word. Remember that God says in the scriptures "Vengeance is Mine; I will repay." "Do not be overcome by evil, but overcome evil with good." (Romans 12:19, 21).
Children of God also offend others. Be prompt to ask for forgiveness. God is no respecter of persons.
8. Read your Bible every day (a few verses or a chapter). Pray daily and ask God to direct you and help you to do and say only those things that please Him. (Psalm 143:8-10, Colossians 3:17 and Ephesians 4:29).
9. Meditate on the Word of God you have read. Memorize any scripture the Spirit lays on your heart. Live according to the Word you have read. Internalize the Word. Pray for grace to be obedient to the Word of God. (Joshua 1:8 James 1:22; Revelation 1:3).
10. As much as possible go to a church or fellowship that believes the whole Bible and the leaders live by what they preach. Always search the scriptures to know if every message you hear is according to the Scriptures. (Hebrews 10:25, Acts 17:11, John 5:39).
11. Tell others about the love of God which you have experienced.

CONCLUSION: Receiving Jesus Christ as your Lord and Savior makes you a child of God. It is a spiritual birth. You are now born again. Jesus says in John 3:3 "Except a man is born again he cannot see the Kingdom of God." It is important for all men to receive Jesus Christ because being born again is our passport to Heaven. John 8:32 says "And you shall know the truth and the truth shall set you free." Jesus is the Truth. Many goats and rams were used in the Old Testament as sacrifice for sin. The blood of those animals only covered the sins of the repentant. We thank Jesus for His blood that washes our sins. John the Baptist on seeing Jesus said in John 1:39 "Behold the Lamb of God who taketh away the sin of the world." Jesus paid the price for all our sins and we have become the children of God by faith in Him. "But if we walk in the light as He is in the light, we have fellowship with one another, and the blood of Jesus Christ, His Son cleanses us from all sin." 1 John 1:7 (NKJV).

After being born again, we have to depend on the Holy Spirit to live a godly life. You now have a passport; you need to have a visa before you can enter into Heaven. I will explain this in the chapter on "Sanctification."

CHAPTER 3

QUIET TIME

Jesus' prayer life was successful because it was always well planned. He habitually prayed in a secluded place. He communed with His Father and prepared Himself for the challenges ahead. "Now in the morning, having risen a long while before daylight, He went out and departed to a solitary place, and there He prayed." (Mark 1:35 NKJV). He has set us an example to follow. There were occasions Jesus had to send His disciples away so that He could spend time alone with the Father. He spent all night in prayers before He chose His disciples. (Luke 6:12-13). As Jesus prayed before He started the day or took up any task, we ought to pray even more.

What is "Quiet Time?"
Luke 6:12; 9:28–29; Psalm 5: 2-3; Psalm 55:17; Mark 1:35; Matthew 14:23.
Christians all over the world refer to a time deliberately set aside to spend in prayer alone with God as "Quite time." It is a time you spend with your heavenly Father. You should make sure that the place you choose is quiet with no distractions or any kind of disturbance. If Jesus rose up early in the morning, you can do the same.

Your phone should be turned off in order to have undisturbed fellowship with God. King David in Psalm 55:17 said that he prayed in the morning, afternoon and at night. You can pray many times in the day or night. The scripture says "pray without ceasing." Please do not miss spending time alone with God. You can choose the time that works best for you but having your "Quiet time" early in the morning gives you the opportunity to handover your challenges of

the day to God and you will receive strength and grace to face the day.
Observing your Quiet time daily gives you the opportunity to worship God as an individual. A family devotion is not regarded as 'Quiet time.' It must be you alone with God. (John 4:24; Psalm 100: 3-5).

Your Quiet time with the Lord gives you the opportunity to hear God speak to you or instruct you. This is why we should not be in a hurry when we come before God in prayer. Psalm 46:10 says "Be still and know that I am God."
It is during your Quiet time that you receive grace and direction for the day. (Psalm 143:8–11; 25:4-5; Hebrews 4:16). You will grow in faith and will have the boldness to declare that God is who He says He is.

Communing with God alone is very important for your spiritual growth. God will continually renew your strength; empower you with the grace and the wisdom to face the battles of life. Proverbs 4:18 says "But the path of the just is as the shining light, that shineth more and more unto the perfect day." (KJV)
Talking with the Lord in your quiet time and Him talking to you through His word or Him speaking to you either audibly or laying it upon your heart, gives you an inexpressible joy. Hearing God speak or knowing when God speaks to you comes with spiritual growth.
If you do not hear Him, believe that He hears you. Remember that the just live by faith. "Therefore I say to you, whatever things you ask when you pray, believe that ye receive them and ye shall have them." (Mark 11:24).

HOW TO HAVE YOUR QUIET TIME

Having a fruitful "Quiet time" is one of the ways a Christian acquires spiritual strength and growth. You should make up your mind to be faithful. Ask the Holy Spirit to help you achieve this goal.

1. **Select a suitable place and time:** Our father Abraham when he was asked to sacrifice his only son Isaac, rose up early in the morning. In Joshua 3:1, Joshua rose early in the morning to prepare his people to go over Jordan. We have already talked about Jesus and King David. Choosing a suitable time and place is important so that you can be consistent. Your closet, your bedroom, living room or anywhere that is devoid of noise will be good if you can have the concentration you need.

2. **What you need:** Have your Bible, a note book, a hymn or chorus book, a pen or pencil. There may be some Bible passages to memorize or a verse you want to ask your Pastor about. Writing memory verses in your notebook or the summary of what you have learnt is always helpful. A comfortable seat in a well-lit environment will help. There are times you may need to stand or walk around to avoid falling asleep during your prayer. The tempter will not want you to pray as you would desire. Please do not give him a chance.

3. **Start with Praising God:** (Psalms 100:4-5; 103:1-3; 150:6; 69:10). The book of Psalms is full of examples on how to praise God. Praise God for who He is, praise Him for what He has done, thank Him for what He has done for you and your family and friends. You may sing hymns or choruses. These help to prepare your heart for a joyous time with the Lord.

4. **Read from the Bible:** Pray for the Spirit of God to illuminate His word and give you understanding. Ask Him to open your spiritual eyes so you can see what He reveals in His word. Only the Holy Spirit can teach the Scriptures. (Psalm 119:11, 18, 34, 105, 130; Romans 8:26-27).

There are many daily devotional books from which you can select the portion of scripture to read for the day. Some daily devotional books are Daily Bread, Daily Manna, Daily Guide, Daily Showers, Every day with Jesus, Open Heaven and YouVersion.
Read the Bible portion over a few times. Meditate on what you have read. (Joshua 1:8; Psalm 1:1-2; 119:1).

The following questions may be useful to help you understand what you have read.
a). Is there anything to learn about God?
b). Is there any instruction to obey or any good example to follow?
c). Is there any warning to heed or any bad example to avoid?
d). Is there any promise to claim?
e). Is there a verse in the portion you have read that you will love to memorize for the day or all week? If any, write it down in your note book.
f). Now that you have received instructions from God, read the brief explanation from the Devotional Book you are using.
g). Pray in the message. Put all that you have learnt in that passage of scripture into prayer. You may use the following as a guide: The passage I read today was from Luke 12:13–21. "The lesson from the rich fool." My prayer on this passage is that God will help me to set my mind on heavenly things. "Heavenly Father, though riches in this world may bring comfort and some pleasure, it is not permanent. May I always remember that all wealth comes from You and that You want me to use it to help the less privileged and for the Kingdom work. Father help me to lay my treasures in heaven so that I will not be like the rich fool in Jesus name. Amen".

Someone else may pray as follows: "Father, You know how I have been struggling to pay my bills and my children's school fees. Please prosper my business. I want to be rich and comfortable in this world because You said that You have come to give us abundant life and that we will not lack any good thing. Lord, give me the wisdom to use my wealth to help those in need and to seek Your face daily and obey Your word. May I not be like the rich fool who did not think of his eternal home in Jesus name. Amen."

Another person may pray like this: "Heavenly Father, I thank You that You have opened my spiritual eyes to see that I have not appreciated that my great wealth is from you. I repent living as if my life is in my hands. Please Father forgive me. I pray for wisdom to plan for my eternal home. My riches have given me sleepless nights and I am suspicious of everyone around me. I totally surrender myself and my riches to You. I do not want to be rich in this world and poor in Heaven like the rich fool. Thank You, Father, for answering my prayer, for I pray in Jesus name. Amen.

h). **Time to make other requests:** (1 Timothy 2:1-3; Philippians 4:6; Matt.7:7; Luke 18:1-8.)

Every believer in Christ is called to be an intercessor. Many people are at a loss as to what to ask God about other people, so they only pray for their immediate family members. The world is in great need and God wants us to intercede on behalf of others. The most important prayer is the prayer for repentance. It is not the will of God that any of us should perish. He wants the world to repent and come to the knowledge of the truth. As you pray for the salvation of the world, use your loved ones as a point of contact. Jesus said in John 3:16–17 "For God so loved the world that He gave His only begotten Son, that whoever believes in Him should not perish but have everlasting life. For God did not send His Son into the world to condemn the world, but that the world through Him might be saved." In John 10:9 Jesus declares, "I am the door. If anyone enters by Me, he will be saved, and will go in and out, and find pasture." (NKJV).

SOME PRAYER POINTS FOR FAMILY DEVOTION, QUIET TIME OR GROUP PRAYERS

1. Praise and thank God before every prayer.
2. Ask God to search your heart and if you have offended Him in any way, ask for forgiveness. God is faithful to His word. He will forgive you. (1 John 1:9).
3. Pray for the unsaved. Those who have not received Jesus as Lord and Savior.
4. Pray for all followers of Christ that they remain faithful to their calling. Remember all the missionaries and the persecuted Christians. Remember their families. Pray for their persecutors that God will reveal Himself to them.
5. Pray for leaders in countries, states, Parliament, offices, homes etc. for God's wisdom to rule aright and that they have the fear of God. Remember their families in your prayers.
6. Pray for families: Pray that God will rule in every home, that there will be peace and unity and that God will guide our children. Pray for provision, protection and that God will grant their heart desires.
7. Pray for all children: The orphans, those with single parents. Remember the youths.
8. Pray for the bereaved, widows, widowers, prisoners, the refugees, the homeless, the jobless, the destitute, the poor and the needy.
9. Pray for all travelers on land, sea and air. Remember the drivers, sea captains and the pilots.
10. Pray for schools and higher institutions: Students, teaching and non-teaching staff, (for excellent performance, love, unity, godly wisdom, success in examinations and promotion for workers).

11. Pray for hospitals: Doctors, nurses, pharmacists and all workers in the hospitals, for (wisdom, provision, love, unity and good health.)
12. Pray for the sick, the aged and the disabled.
13. Pray for those who have court cases, for God's intervention.
14. Pray for workers in all industries, farmers, business men and women.
15. Pray for Soldiers, Firefighters, Police and Emergency workers.
16. Pray for all citizens to obey their rulers in all that pleases the Lord.
17. Pray for people in war zones and areas or countries affected by natural disaster.

CHAPTER 4

WHAT IS PRAYER?

Prayer is communing with God. When we pray, we talk to God and God talks to us through His word. Prayer is very important in the life of a Christian. Men began to call on the name of Lord in Genesis 4:26. The disciples of Jesus asked Him to teach them how to pray because John the Baptist taught his followers how to pray. (Luke 11:1). Jesus said "that men ought always to pray and not to faint" Luke 18:1. God created man for His glory and to praise Him. (Isaiah 43:7,21) God is our Creator. He wants us to show our total dependence on Him. We cannot do anything right without Him.

God is our Father and recognizes us as His children, when we flee from sin and obey His commands. (2 Cor. 6:17-18; 1 John 3:1-2). God, as our Father wants to have fellowship with us. 1 John 1:3b says, "truly our fellowship is with the Father, and with His son Jesus Christ." A child that has a good relationship with his father will spend time with him. He will learn so much from his father and soon begin to behave like his father. When we form the habit of spending time daily with our Heavenly Father in prayer, studying and obeying His word, we will become more like Him. This is a sure way of having the mind of Christ.

JESUS TEACHES US HOW TO PRAY:
Luke 11:1 -4; Matthew 6:9-13.

In response to the request of His disciples, Jesus gave them a model or pattern of prayer. Many Christians refer to this model prayer as "the Lord's prayer." The real prayer of Jesus is in John chapter 17. In the model prayer, Jesus indicates areas of concern that should occupy a Christian's prayer: The prayer contains six petitions: three are concerned with the holiness and will of God; three are concerned with our personal needs.

Our Father which at in Heaven: Prayer involves the worship of our heavenly Father. Let your mind focus on the fact that you cannot see Him but you know that He is with you. Through Jesus, we can have intimacy with the God who loves us and cares for us. God is holy and will always oppose sin. As our Heavenly Father, He can punish as well as bless, withhold as well as give, act with justice as well as mercy. How He responds to His children, depends on our faith in and our obedience to Him.

Hallowed be thy name: Our greatest concern in our prayers is to reverence God and hallow His name. Praising, glorifying and exalting God is very important. (Psalms 34:1; 100:3-5). Worship Him for who He is and praise Him for His goodness. Remember all He has done for you. Count your blessings one by one. In our prayers and daily walk, we must be concerned with the reputation of God. To do something that brings scandal on the Lord's name is a great sin and gives the unbelievers an occasion to dishonor God.

Thy Kingdom Come: We must pray for the spiritual presence and manifestation of the Kingdom of God. This includes believers receiving the power of the Holy Ghost to destroy the works of Satan, heal the sick, save the lost and promote righteousness. (1 John 3:8; Luke 19:10).

Thy will be done on earth as it is in Heaven: To pray "Thy will be done" means we sincerely desire God's will and purpose to be fulfilled in our lives and the lives of our families, according to His eternal plan. We know the will of God because it is revealed in His word, the Bible. The Holy Spirit also teaches us all truth. (Romans 8:4 -5; John 14:26). The will of God is accomplished when we pray for God's righteousness to be seen in all who call on His name. (Matthew 6:33; Romans 14:17).

Give us this day our daily bread: Here you pray for your individual daily needs. Do not be anxious about anything. Pray to your Father. He knows your needs. (Philippians 4:6; Matt. 7:7; Phil. 4:19).

And forgive us our debts as we forgive our debtors: There is a condition for our prayers to be answered. If we do not forgive those who offend us, our own sins will not be forgiven by God. Think about this. No offence is too little to be overlooked. (Matt.6:14-15; Hebrews 9:14; Ephesians 4:32; 1 John 1:9).

And lead us not into temptation but deliver us from evil: All believers are the special objects of Satan's enmity and evil purpose. We must pray for God's protection and deliverance from the enemy's power and schemes. (Luke 11:26; 1 Peter 5:8, 2 Pet. 2:9; Psalm 91:3).

For thine is the Kingdom, and the power, and the glory forever. Amen: Praise God because all the power and glory belong to Him. He alone has the power to answer your prayers. He is the God of all flesh; there is nothing too hard for Him.

The model prayer is short but contains a lot of lessons. Jesus spent a long time talking to His Father in prayer. He had night prayers as well. (Luke 6:12).

To follow the pattern of the prayer Jesus taught His disciples we learn that **1.** We start every prayer by praising God. **2.** We ask for forgiveness of sins and if there are people, we have not forgiven, we should endeavor to forgive them. **3.** We should ask for our daily needs. Intercede for our family, church members; different organizations and colleagues. Pray as the Spirit leads. **4.** Pray for our protection. **5.** Praise and thank God for answered prayers.

Praying in the name of Jesus: The name of Jesus is a matchless name. It is a name that is glorious, wonderful and higher than any other name. A name above all names. A powerful name that makes the kingdom of darkness to quake. The name that heals and delivers. The name that raises the dead.

At the mention of the name of Jesus every knee shall bow whether in heaven or on earth or under the sea.

As Jesus ascended into heaven, He gave us His name to use for our protection and to challenge the enemy of our souls. He commanded us to pray in His name and that our prayers will be answered. Read the following scriptures and understand why you should pray only in the name of Jesus.

1 John 14: 13 – 14
2 John 15: 7
3 John 15:16
4 John 16: 23, 24, 26
5 Mark 16:17 – 18
6 Colossians 3:17
7 Ephesians 5:20
8 Hebrews 7:25-26; Romans 8:34

Praying in the name of Jesus is one of the privileges of a child of God. Hebrews 7:25 reads "Therefore He is able also to save forever those who come to God through Him, since He always lives to intercede and intervene on their behalf (with God)." (Amplified Study Bible). Do not be deceived, no human or angel can intervene on your behalf. Only Jesus, the Lamb that was slain, our Mediator, the one that paid the price for our sins, He only can intervene on our behalf.

CONCLUSION: God loves to have fellowship with His children. It is only through prayer that we can experience that Father-son relationship. Pray and believe God for answers to your petition. Jesus said to the people He healed "It is unto you according to your faith." Pray and believe. God has given us the Holy Spirit to help us pray aright. (Romans 8:26). Many have the testimony of answers to their prayers. He will honor His word. He has promised that if we pray according to His will, He answers us. (1 John 5:14).

CHAPTER 5

WATER BAPTISM

The importance of water baptism: Water baptism is the next step after salvation through repentance and faith in Christ. It is an important foundation for the Christian life. Water Baptism is one of immersion "In the name of the Father, and of the Son, and of the Holy Ghost." (Matt. 28:19; 3:13-17; Mark 16:15-16; Acts 2:38; 19:1-6; Romans 6:4-5). Jesus commanded His disciples to baptize their followers, Christians are bound to obey the commands of Jesus. "If you love me, keep my commandments." (John 14:15).

What does the word "Baptize" mean?
John 3:23; Mark 1:10; Acts 8:38–39.
The word "baptize" is from the Greek word "baptizo" which means "dip" or "immerse". The descriptions of baptisms in the New Testament suggest that people went down into the water to be immersed. Both Jesus and Philip were immersed into the water.
Other water baptisms were not specific but because immersion was the Jewish way of identification or initiation into the fellowship, I believe that all followers in the early Church were immersed in water. I will want to do what Jesus did.

The Baptism of John: Mark 1:5; Matt. 3:1–2; Luke 3: 8–18.
The Jews practiced water baptism as a traditional act of purification to initiate converts into Judaism. John, the son of Zacharias and Elizabeth was in the wilderness baptizing his followers. He fulfilled the scripture in Isaiah 40:3, "The voice of one crying in the wilderness: Prepare the way of the Lord; Make straight in the desert, a highway for our God." (NKJV). John was a fearless preacher who declared God's word with boldness.

He told the people their sins to their faces. Many who heard his preaching repented of their evil deeds. They confessed their sins and believed in the coming Messiah. John baptized all his converts. This earned him the name 'John the Baptist'. John the Baptist's converts received forgiveness for their sins because of their faith in the promised Anointed one. They were saved by faith not by baptism. John's baptism was a public expression of repentance. It made them the followers of John or John's disciples.

Jesus was baptized by John: Jesus was baptized by John for the following reasons; **1.** "To fulfill all righteousness" Matt. 3:15; (compare this with Leviticus 16:24; Jesus is Our High Priest). **2.** To identify Himself with the sinners He had come to save. Jesus had no sin to repent of before being baptized. (2 Cor. 5:21) Identifying with sinners and eating with them was one of His methods of reaching out to the people. **3.** To associate Himself with John the Baptist's ministry as the forerunner of the Messiah (John 1:23, 32-33) in fulfillment of what was prophesied by Isaiah (Isaiah 40:3) and (Malachi 3:1).

The baptism of Jesus gave us the privilege of observing the Triune God at work; The Holy Trinity. In the Old Testament the Spirit of God descended on individuals and empowered them to lead the people of God. In Zechariah 4:6, the scripture says, "Not by might, not by power but by my Spirit, says the Lord of hosts." Jesus, as man needed the infilling of the Holy Spirit to start His ministry. Matt. 3:16-17 reads "After Jesus was baptized, He came up immediately out of the water; and behold the heavens were opened, and he (John) saw the Spirit of God descending as a dove and lighting on Him (Jesus), and behold, a voice from Heaven said, "This is My beloved Son, in whom I am well-pleased and delighted!" (Psalm 2:7; Isaiah 42:1 Amplified Study Bible).

God the Father spoke from Heaven, God the Son was coming up from the water after being baptized and God the Holy Spirit descended like a dove. The Blessed Trinity was at work at the baptism of Jesus.

Who should be baptized?
Mark 16: 16; Acts 2: 38, 41; Matt. 28:19.
Only those who believe in the Lord Jesus Christ and have repented for their sins are qualified for water baptism. It is mandatory that a believer in Christ must submit himself for water baptism according to the scriptures. Any responsible Christian who is in right standing with the Lord can baptize. Paul was baptized by one described as a "disciple." (Acts 9:10-18).

What is the significance of water baptism? Luke 12:8 – 9.
Water baptism declares that you are a follower of Christ. It is a public confession of your faith in, and commitment to Jesus Christ. It is a symbol of your new life as a Christian. It is an outward symbol of the commitment you made in your heart that has to be followed through and lived out on a daily basis. It is like a wedding ring you wear to show that you are married but the commitment is in your heart. It is like an enlisted soldier putting on the uniform. (Galatians 3:27).

We bury the old life and we rise to walk in a new life. The river or pool signifies the grave, and your body, the corpse. Your old self has been crucified with Christ. This old life is buried in the act of baptism. Christ died and rose from the dead. As you are buried with Him in baptism, your rising up out of the river or pool signifies your resurrection in newness of life. In baptism, you die with Christ and rise with Him. (Galatians 2:20; Rom.6:1–11).

Conclusion
Water baptism is mandatory not optional if you are privileged to live after being saved. The thief on the cross who repented died on the same day and had a place in heaven. Jesus commanded us to be baptized in water as a public declaration that we are His disciples. If we deny Him, He will deny us before His Father. Remember that you are baptized "into Christ" and not into a "denomination." (1 Corinthians 12:13 – 14).

Water baptism is for only those who have repented and confessed their sins to God and received Jesus as their Lord and Savior. Baptizing children before they know what "sin" is, is not scriptural. Children are not accountable for their conduct until they reach the age of accountability. The age of accountability varies. The message is "Repent and be baptized." (Acts 2:38). Repent and believe the gospel." (Mark 1:15c).

If you were baptized before you gave your life to Christ, you need to be baptized according to the scripture. In Acts 19:1 - 5, those who were baptized "into John's baptism" had to be baptized in the name of the Lord, Jesus Christ. Some denominations teach that water baptism washes away our sins. This is false teaching. Only the Blood of Jesus washes our sins away. 1 John 1:7c, says "the Blood of Jesus Christ, His Son cleanses us from all sin." Hebrews. 9:22 says "without the shedding of the blood there is no remission or forgiveness of sin." It is the blood not water that washes away our sins.

CHAPTER 6

SANCTIFICATION, THE SECOND WORK OF GRACE

Teaching the doctrines: Matt. 28:18–20; Isaiah 28: 9-10; 1 Timothy 4:16.

In the last chapter of the book of Revelation, the Bible instructs us not to add to or subtract from the word of God. Every pastor, priest or teacher of the word of God must be diligent to obey God's instructions. The Bible verses listed above instruct us to teach the whole doctrine and live by them. Isaiah says to teach it "precept upon precept, line upon line." 1 Timothy 4:16 says "Take heed to yourself and to the doctrine, continue in them, for in doing this you will save both yourself and those who hear you." (NKJV). All teachers of the word must teach their congregation about "holiness" which is also known as "sanctification." In Hebrews 12:14, the scripture says, "Follow peace with all men, and holiness, without which no man shall see the Lord." (KJV). Holiness is required before you can see God. You need a valid passport and a visa to enter another country. To enter the Kingdom of God, (heaven) you need a valid passport (genuine salvation) and a visa (sanctification or holiness).

Our spiritual race to heaven can be illustrated as a student who is admitted in a school (salvation). He gets the school uniform (water baptism). In the school you are taught many subjects and you move from one grade to the other as you are being prepared for your final examination. (You read the Bible and obey the word. You grow spiritually and pass the final examination of death or of rapture.) At the end of your final year in school you get a certificate.

At the end of life, you are either in heaven with a "crown of righteousness" or in hell with the "fire that will never quench."

Your success or failure in school, depends on how hard you worked and the interest you had in learning.

In the spiritual race, God gives us His grace, the Bible, ministers and teachers of the word. All He wants from us is to believe what the Bible teaches and do it. Faith is important for any child of God to be able to run this race, that is why "the just shall live by faith." Hebrews 11:6 says "But without faith it is impossible to please Him, for He who comes to God, must believe that He is, and that He is a rewarder of those who diligently seek Him." Paul prayed in 1 Thess. 5:23 that God's peace will sanctify the believers and preserve them blameless at the coming of the Lord.

What is Sanctification?

The word "sanctification" or "to sanctify" is used in the Bible to mean:
1. To set apart for God's use. It means to dedicate or consecrate. You can consecrate yourself to work for God. You can dedicate yourself to accomplish a task for God. You may dedicate a car or a house to the church, even your tithes. (Exodus 13:1-2), "The Lord spoke unto Moses saying, sanctify unto me all the first born, whatever opens the womb among the children of Israel, both of man and beast; it is Mine".

2. Sanctification also means to make holy or pure, to be free from sin, to be perfect. God is holy and He commands us to be holy. "Be ye holy for I am Holy" (1 Peter 1:16). God will not command us to be holy if He does not know that we can be holy. He does not expect us to be as holy as the angels but as holy as Father Abraham, Elijah, Elisha, Job, Apostle Paul and other men with a nature like ours, who ran this spiritual race and made it across the finish line. In Genesis 17:1, God said to Abraham "walk before me and be perfect or blameless." Sanctification is not for sinners. You must be saved, then, you can pray to be sanctified.

If you do not speak in tongues but you are holy; you will make Heaven. If you do not understand the whole Bible but you are holy; you will make Heaven. If you do not memorize Bible verses but you are holy; you have a place in Heaven. All you need to make Heaven, is to be saved and live a holy or blameless life. Hebrews 12:14b says "without holiness no man shall see the Lord." Sanctification is the second work of grace in a believer's life.

Some erroneous doctrines that deceive the people:
Romans 5:1; Colossians 1:19-23.

1. **Some confuse Justification with Sanctification:** Justification in the Bible, is the freedom we receive when we give our lives to Christ. God receives us and treats us as if we had never sinned. Romans 5:1 says, "Therefore, having been justified by faith, we have peace with God through our Lord Jesus Christ."

2. **Some teach that being born again is gradual:** They believe and teach that as you go to church, read the Bible, confess your sins and try to do some good works, then you are saved. Wrong doctrine!!! In real life you do not deliver the leg, then the hand, and then the head. The baby is delivered once. For the spiritual birth, there must be a day you recognize that you are a sinner and also a candidate for hell. If you repent of your sins, confess them to God, determine to forsake those sins and then ask Jesus to come and dwell in your heart, you will be saved. "For whoever calls on the name of the Lord will be saved." (Romans 10:13). "That Christ may dwell in your hearts through faith." (Ephesians 3:17a) Salvation is the first step to following Christ. Faith in God plays an important role in your salvation.

3. **Some teach that no man can be holy and that holiness is a gradual process:** We do not grow into sanctification or holiness but we can grow in sanctification or holiness. In Luke 1: 6, Elizabeth and Zacharias were counted as holy; "They were both righteous before God,

walking in all the commandments and ordinances of the Lord, blameless." Job had the same testimony. In Job 1:8, God said to Satan, "Have you considered My servant Job, that there is none like him on earth, a blameless and upright man, one who fears God and shuns evil?" (NKJV).

God wants us to be holy so that we can have fellowship with Him for He is holy. Some denominations do not teach "Sanctification" as a doctrine to be studied, believed and practiced. John Wesley once said, "that there is no holiness in any church where "holiness" is not taught." The truth is that your ignorance will not be excused by God because the Bible is there for all to read and ask questions. You are privileged if you are in a church or fellowship where the whole Bible is taught line upon line, precept upon precept.

God made provision for our sanctification: Leviticus 16:27; Deut. 30:6; Matt. 5:6; John 17:17; 1 Thess. 4:3,7 -8; Titus: 2:13-14; Hebrews 13:12-13; 1 Pet.1: 2; James 1:6.

Just as God made provision for our salvation with the blood of Jesus to cleanse our sins, so He also made provision for our sanctification. In the Old Testament, "the bull for the sin offering and the goat for the sin offering, whose blood was brought in to make atonement in the holy place, shall be carried outside the camp." (Lev.16:27). Jesus our Lord and Master, our Perfect Sacrifice fulfilled this scripture when He was crucified outside the city or outside the gate. Hebrews 13:12 says "Therefore, Jesus also, that He might sanctify the people with His own blood, suffered outside the gate." Titus 2: 13-14 says, "Looking for the blessed hope and glorious appearing of our great God and Savior Jesus Christ, who gave Himself for us, that He might redeem us from every lawless deed and purify for Himself His own special people, zealous for good works." (NKJV).

The agents of Sanctification: The Holy Spirit uses the word of God to work out our Sanctification just as He does for our salvation. The word points us to Jesus and His blood. The word also gives us faith to believe that Jesus is our Perfect Sacrifice. He is our Sanctifier. Just as we are saved by grace, we are also sanctified by grace. So, the means of grace that gets a believer into this experience are: (1) The word of God (John 15:3); (2) The blood of Jesus (Hebrews 13:12–13); (3) Faith in the Lord. (Acts 26:18; Romans 10:17); (4) God Himself and the Spirit of God. (1 Thess. 5:23).

The need for sanctification after Salvation:
Genesis 6: 5; Jeremiah 17: 9.
At salvation, the blood of Jesus cleanses us from all sins but the tendency to sin still remains. This desire to sin is sometimes referred to as the Adamic nature. The root of sin is the Adamic nature. The Bible teaches that the heart of man is deceitful and desperately wicked. This is why we need God to sanctify our hearts. Salvation is like a huge tree which is cut down but the root is still in the ground. When the rain falls the tree will start to grow again. The root of that tree needs to be dug out before the tree can stop growing. After being saved, the root of sin, the desire to sin needs to be dug out. This happens when the heart is sanctified. If the desire for sin is not taken away the believer may be tempted to go back to those sins he had forsaken.

Jesus' disciples needed to be blameless, pure, holy or sanctified:
Jesus said in Luke 10:20 that the names of His disciples were written in Heaven. I understand this to mean that they were born again but they were still selfish, high minded and ambitious. Jesus had to correct them and prayed for them.

(a). In Matt. 20: 20–24, the mother of James and John wanted high position for her sons. These sons may have asked their mother to intervene, (seeking position). Verse 24 says that when the other ten heard it, they were greatly displeased with the two brothers, (anger and jealousy). These sins can only be rooted out through the second work of grace; "Sanctification."

(b). In Luke 22:24-27, the disciples argued about greatness. They wanted to know who was the greatest among them, (seeking position/title). Jesus had to correct them. They needed sanctification.

(c). In Matt. 15:22–23, the Canaanite woman needed help. Jesus did not answer her. The disciples said to Jesus, "send her away, for she cries out after us." The disciples had no pity on her. They were judgmental and racists. They needed pure hearts.

(d). In Matt. 26:7–12, the woman with the alabaster flask of very costly fragrant oil poured the oil on Jesus' head as He sat at the table. When the disciples saw it, they were indignant, saying "Why this waste? The disciples were angry. They needed sanctified hearts.

(e). In Luke 9:51–56, the Samaritans did not receive Jesus as He came into one of the villages. When His disciples, James and John saw this, they said "Lord, do you want us to command fire to come down from heaven and consume them, just as Elijah did?" The two disciples quoted the scripture to support their evil plan. They wanted to use their authority and power in a wrong way. They nursed the spirit of revenge. A clean heart was what they needed.

(f). In Mark 14: 46-50. When Jesus was arrested, one of the disciples cut off the ear of the enemy. (Revenge, judgmental spirit and inflicting pain without remorse). He needed a new heart.

Why is 'Sanctification' important?
The experience of being holy, pure, blameless, perfect or sanctified is important because:

1. **God commanded it:**
 Leviticus 20:7; 1 Peter 1:14–16. God said "Be ye holy."

2. **God demands it:** In Genesis 17:1, Abram was 99 years old when God said to him, "I am the Almighty God, walk before Me and be thou perfect."

3. **Holiness is the nature of God:** In Leviticus 19:2, God said to the children of Israel, "Ye shall be holy: for I the Lord your God am holy."

4. **It is difficult to maintain a consistent walk with God, without being holy:** Leviticus 11:43–45; 26: 23–24; Amos 3:3.

5. **Sanctification helps a believer to love God deeply:** "And the Lord your God will circumcise your heart and the hearts of your descendants (that is, He will remove the desire to sin from your heart), so that you will love the Lord your God with all your heart and all your soul so that you may live as a recipient of His blessing." (Deut. 30:6 Amplified Study Bible) Ezekiel 11:19-20.

6. **It helps you to obey God with a proper motive:**
Duet 10:12-13, 16 says, "And now Israel, what does the Lord your God require of you, but to fear the Lord your God, to walk in all His ways and to love Him, to serve the Lord your God with all your heart and with all your soul, and to keep the commandments of the Lord and His statutes which I command you today for your good? (16) Therefore, circumcise the foreskin of your heart, and be stiff-necked no longer."

7. **In character and conduct, sanctification makes us holy like our Heavenly Father:** "Therefore you shall be perfect, just as your Father in heaven is perfect." (Matt. 5:48) "Let this mind be in you which was also in Christ Jesus." (Philippians 2:5).

8. **Sanctification brings us into unity with other believers:** Jesus prayed for our sanctification. "Sanctify them by Your truth. Your word is truth." (John 17:17). And in verse 21, Jesus prayed, "that they all may be one, as You, Father, are in Me, and I in You; that they also may be one in Us, that the world may believe that You sent Me."

How to become "Sanctified."
Sanctification is the second work of grace. It is the gift of God. Jesus is our Sanctifier. To be sanctified, you must be born again and know the "truth" which will set you free, (John 8:32). Jesus prayed for our sanctification in John 17:17, 20.
Separate yourself from the world: (2 Corinthians 6:17; Isaiah 52:11; Romans. 12:1 – 2.)
Make peace with people: Settle all quarrels, make any restitution. (Ephesians 4:31 – 32; Luke 19:8).
Consecrate all to God: Surrender all, your whole being, talent, money, ambition to God.
Desire and hunger for it: "Blessed are those who hunger and thirst after righteousness, for they shall be filled." (Matt. 5:6 NKJV). Psalm 42:1- 2 says, "As the deer pants for the water brooks, so pants my soul for You, O God. My soul thirsts for God, for the living God. When shall I come and appear before God?" Psalm 63:1-8
Pray for it: Ezekiel 36:26-27; 11: 19-20; Matt. 7:7-8; Luke 11:9-10; 1 Thess. 4:3,7; Jeremiah 33:3. Pray and believe that God will answer your prayers: 1 Thess. 5:24; Mark 11:24; 1 John 5:14; Acts 15:8-9; Romans 1:17.

The benefits of sanctification:
(a). You will know God more and enjoy deeper peace of God.
(b). You will have a pure motive for doing things. You will be free from murmuring, criticizing other people and doing things that please just you.
(c). You will love God sincerely and will not complain about God's demands. You will be ready and willing to do everything for God. (Pay your tithes, help the less privileged, always willing to serve others.)
(d). You will have pure and sacrificial love for believers and unbelievers; 1Corinthians 13:4-8.
(e). You will be entirely yielded to God. Prophet Isaiah was ready to obey God. He said to God, "here am I, send me."
(f). Many people will respect you because you only do the things that please God.
(g). Your affections are set on the things of heaven. Colossians 3:1-2; Psalms 73:25.
(h). You are sensitive to the leading and prodding of the Spirit.
(i). You will show Christlike humility. Philippians 2:5-8.
(j). You will be united with Christ and His church. You will be united in life style, doctrine and you will love all God's word. John 17:21-23; Isaiah 52: 7-8; 57:15; 62:2.
(k). A sanctified believer has the assurance of a place in heaven because he has the visa into the Kingdom of God. Hebrews 12:14 says "Follow peace with all men, and holiness, without which no man shall see the Lord." (KJV).

Conclusion
I will conclude with an excerpt from my favorite daily devotional guide, (Daily Manna). "Man's uprightness and righteous living does God no favor. It does not add to or remove anything from His person. When people understand this truth, they will not continue to think that they do God a favor by repenting and living a holy life. It is astonishing when some people begin to commit sin recklessly because they feel God has disappointed them. Just because the answer to their prayer did not come early enough, they feel they can "punish" God by backsliding. How foolish! Who will face the punishment for such sinful lifestyle; God or such individuals?

It is true that the Lord is pleased with our holy living and delights in it but ultimately, the benefits of holy living is ours. We reap the benefits of divine favor when we choose to obey and please Him. Therefore, God's call and command for us to live holy lives is for our ultimate good, not His. It is wise then to heed such call and daily ask for grace to please Him."
"BE YE HOLY FOR I AM HOLY" SAYS OUR GOD. Let holiness unto the Lord be our watch word and song. The grace of God saved you. The grace of God will also sanctify you. It is grace upon grace. Ask and receive. It shall be unto you according to your faith.

CHAPTER 7

THE HOLY SPIRIT, A DIVINE PERSONALITY

Who is the Holy Spirit?
The Holy Spirit is a Divine personality. He shares the Godhead with the Father and the Son. (2 Corinthians 13:14). He is the third Person in the Trinity. Believers must honor, worship, listen to and have fellowship with Him. He is called the Holy Ghost, (Matt. 28:19) the Spirit of your Father, (Matt. 10:20) the Spirit of Christ, (1 Peter 1: 11) the Spirit of wisdom, (Ephesians 1:17) the Spirit of grace, (Hebrews 10:29) the Spirit of Glory, (1Peter 4:14) the Spirit of God, (1 Corinthians 3:16) the Spirit of the Living God, (2 Corinthians 3:3) the Spirit of Holiness, (Romans 1:4) the Spirit of Life, (Romans 8:2) the Spirit of truth, (John 15:26) The Eternal Spirit, (Hebrews 9:14). (Bible quotations are from KJV). The Holy Spirit is eternal, omnipotent, omnipresent and omniscient. He illuminates and inspires the Holy Scriptures. He convicts sinners of their sins. He is the Great Teacher, Comforter, Guide and our partner in time of need.

What are the symbols of the Holy Spirit?
The symbols of the Holy Spirit in the Bible are:
(a). Water: John 7:38–39.
(b). Wind: John 3:8.
(c). Seal: Ephesians 1:13.
(d). Dove: Matt. 3:16.
(e). Fire: Acts 2:3 – 4.

THE WORK OF THE HOLY SPIRIT

"The Holy Spirit in relation to creation: The Holy Spirit was active in creation and imparts life into all creatures. (Genesis 1: 2; Job 33: 4; Psalm 104:30.) In Genesis 1:26a, God said, "Let Us make man in Our image, after Our likeness."

THE WORK OF THE HOLY SPIRIT IN RELATION TO JESUS CHRIST

Jesus was conceived in Mary by the Spirit: Matt. 1:18; 20-23; Luke. 1: 34-35.

Jesus performed miracles by the power of the Holy Spirit: Isaiah 61:1; Matt. 12:28; Acts 10:38.

Jesus will baptize believers with the Holy Spirit: Matt. 3:11; Mark 1: 8; Luke 3:16; John 1:33; Acts 1: 4 – 5; 2:1-4; 11:16.

Jesus was raised from the dead by the Spirit: Romans 1:3 – 4; 8:11.

Jesus received the Spirit from the Father: Acts 2:33.

Jesus is glorified by the Spirit: John 16: 13 – 14.

Jesus is revealed to believers by the Spirit: John 16:13 -14.

Jesus offered Himself on the cross through the Spirit: Hebrews 9:14.

THE WORK OF THE HOLY SPIRIT IN RELATION TO THE CHURCH

The Holy Spirit dwells in the Church as His temple: 1 Corinthians 3:16; Ephesians. 2:22.

The Spirit is poured out like rain upon the church: Acts 1:5; 2:1-4; Hosea 6:3, Joel 2:28.
The Spirit speaks to the church: Revelation 2:7,11, 17, 27; 3:6,13,22.

The Spirit creates fellowship, unites and gives gifts to the church: 2 Corinthians 13:14; Philippians 2:1; Ephesians 4:4; 1 Corinthians 12:13; Romans 12:6-8.

The Spirit appoints leaders and works through Spirit filled people: Numbers 27:18; Judges 6:34; Acts 6: 3,5,8; 8: 6-12; 20:28; Ephesians 4:11.

The Spirit empowers preachers and directs the missionary work: 1 Corinthians 2:4; Acts 8:29,39; 16: 6-7; 20:23.

The Spirit guards the church against error, warns the church of apostasy: 2 Timothy 1:14; 1 Timothy 4:1.

The Spirit equips the church for Spiritual warfare: Ephesians 6:10-18.

The Spirit promotes righteousness in the church: Romans 14:17; Ephesians 2:21-22; 3:16-21; 1 Thess. 4:7-8.

The Holy Spirit convicts us of sin and regenerates us:
John 3:5-6; 16: 7-11; 14: 17; 20: 22; Acts 2:37; Romans 8:9; 2 Cor. 3:6; Titus.3: 5.

The Holy Spirit imparts God's love to us and, makes us realize that God is our Father: Romans 5: 5; 8:14-16; Galatians 4:6.

The Holy Spirit reveals Christ and God's truth to us: Nehemiah 9:20 John 14:16-17,26; 15:26; 16:13-15; 1 Corinthians 2: 9-16.

The Holy Spirit enables us to distinguish truth from error and incorporates us into the church: 1 John 4: 1-3; 1 Corinthians 12:13.

Jesus Christ baptizes us into the Holy Spirit and He fills us:
Judges 14:19; Matt. 3:11; Mark 1: 8; John 1:33; Luke 1:15, 41,67, Acts 1:4-5; 2: 4; 4: 8, 31; 6:3-5; 7:55; 11:16; Ephesians 5:19.

The Holy Spirit gives us power and boldness to witness:
Luke1:15-17; 24: 47-49; Acts 1:8; 4:31; 6:9-10; 19:6; Romans 9:1-3.

The Holy Spirit gives us special gifts, visions and prophecy:
Joel 2:28-29; Mark 16:17-18; Acts 2:17-18; 10:9-22; 1 Cor. 1:7; 12: 7-11; 14:1-5, 21-25; 1 Peter 4:10-11.

The Holy Spirit develops His fruit in us and enables us to live a holy life: Ezekiel 11:19-20; Psalm 51:10-12; 143:10; Romans 8:4-10; 14:17; 1 Corinthians 13; Galatians 5: 16-18, 22-23, 25; Philippians 2:12-13; 1 Thess. 1:6; 2 Thess. 2:13; 1 Peter 1:2.

The Holy Spirit frees us from the power of sin and enables us to fight Satan with the word: Romans 8:2; Ephesians 3:16; 6:17.

The Holy Spirit gives us comfort and encouragement and enables us to speak at difficult moments: Matt.10:17-20; Mark 13:11; Luke 12:11-12; John 14:17-18, 26-27; Acts 9:31.

The Holy Spirit helps us to pray and enables us to worship: John 4:23-24; Acts 4: 23-24; 10:46; Romans 8:26; Ephesians 5:18-19; 6:18; Philippians 3:3; Jude 20.

The Holy Spirit gives life to our mortal bodies and makes us yearn for Christ's return: Romans 8:11, 23; Revelation 22:20.

THE HOLY SPIRIT IN RELATION TO SINNERS

The Holy Spirit convicts sinners of sin, righteousness and judgment: John 16: 7-11.

The Holy Spirit commissions believers to proclaim the gospel to sinners: Acts 1:8; 2:17,21; 4:31; 11:12-18; 13: 1-4.

The Holy Spirit reveals the saving truth of the gospel: Luke 4:18-19; John 15:26-27; Acts 4:8; 11:15,18; 14:3; 1 Cor. 2:4, 12; 1 Thess. 1:5." (Life in the Spirit Study Bible).

Blasphemy against the Holy Spirit:
We all need the Holy Spirit in everything we do. The Bible warns us in Ephesians 4:30, not to grieve the Holy Spirit. In Matt. 12: 31-32 Jesus said, "Wherefore I say unto you, all manner of sin and blasphemy shall be forgiven unto men: but the blasphemy against the Holy Ghost shall not be forgiven unto men. (32) And whosoever speaks a word against the Son of man, it shall be forgiven him: but whosoever speaks against the Holy Ghost, it shall not be forgiven him, either in this world or in the world to come." (NKJV). Some Leaders in different church denominations have dishonored God in their pursuit of wealth and have led their young followers (new converts) and unbelievers to blaspheme the Holy Spirit. These leaders use occultic powers to perform miracles, they speak in tongues, but it is not from the Lord. Unfortunately, some of their members are magnetized by this false behavior. This exhibition of false spirituality makes it difficult for the spiritually blind to separate themselves from their evil deeds. They become easy prey. Blasphemy against the Holy Spirit involves attributing the authority and power of God to Satan.

If a genuine minister of God, through the anointing of the Holy Ghost performs the miracle of healing the sick or opening the eyes of the blind and you say and believe that it is by the power of Satan that he performed that miracle, you have blasphemed the Holy Spirit. If you continue with that attitude, your heart may be hardened, (apostasy). You will have a depraved mind which sees evil as good and good as evil. The Holy Spirit, who convicts people of sin, will have no choice but to leave you to your fate. This is why the sin against the Holy Spirit will not be forgiven in this world or in the world to come. Only the Holy Spirit convicts us of our sin. (1Corinthians 12:3) "Wherefore I give you to understand, that no man speaking by the Spirit of God calleth Jesus accursed: and that no man can say that Jesus is Lord, but by the Holy Ghost." The good news is, if you still want to be forgiven of your sins and you are willing to repent and be saved, you have not committed the unpardonable sin.

Conclusion:

We need the Holy Spirit to always lead and direct us. We have learnt about His work in relation to creation, the church, the believers and the sinners. The Lord will help us to flee from sin so we can obey His word. 1 Thess. 5:19-20 Says "Quench not the Spirit. Despise not prophesying." The Bible encourages us to test all prophetic utterances (which includes the teaching of the word of God) whether or not they are in line with the scriptures. Reject any prophesy or teaching which is not according to God's word.

May the fire of the Holy Spirit kindle in our hearts so we can know Him more and be obedient to His calling in Jesus name. Amen.

CHAPTER 8

THE HOLY SPIRIT BAPTISIM

Man cannot carry out supernatural activities without the enabling power of God. In the Old Testament, men like Elijah, Gideon, Samson, Balaam and a few more had the Spirit upon them to accomplish the work assigned to them by God. (Numbers 24:2; Judges 6:34). However, they did not enjoy the continuous abiding presence of the Holy Spirit. God in His love decided to give us the Holy Spirit to dwell in believers in the new covenant. (John 14:17). This is one of the privileges of the death and resurrection of Jesus Christ.

The Holy Spirit plays an important role in our salvation because He convicts us of our sin and reminds us of the sins we have committed, so we can confess them. The scripture says that no one calls Jesus Lord without the Holy Spirit. The Holy Spirit guides and guards the believer in Christ. He wants to empower you for the work of the Kingdom. This power is given when you are baptized with the Holy Spirit. Always remember that sanctification is for purity. The baptism with the Holy Spirit is for power.

Who is qualified to be baptized with the Holy Spirit?

The Holy Spirit Baptism is for all born again believers who have set themselves apart to obey God. It is for those who are pure in heart, blameless and sanctified. It is for those who have put their hands to the plough and will not look back. (Luke 9:62). This baptism with the Holy Spirit was first experienced by 120 disciples of Jesus in the upper room in Acts 1:13-14; 2:2-3. In Acts 1:14, the Bible says, "These all continued with one accord in prayer and supplication with the women, and Mary the mother of Jesus, and with His brethren." This highlights the humility of the mother of Jesus. She waited in the upper room with the other disciples! She was also a disciple of Christ.

She was obedient to all the rules and needed to wait for the power from on high. If the mother of Jesus waited for this power, we also should desire it. In the previous chapter we read that Jesus healed the sick and cast out demons by the power of the Holy Spirit. All believers need this power. Some denominations teach that the Holy Spirit baptism was for the disciples at Pentecost.

The promise of the baptism in the Holy Spirit is for us and our children and as many as our God shall call. (Acts 2:39). The out pouring of the Holy Spirit is promised to all flesh and to all who are pure and desire the Spirit power. (Isaiah 44:3; Ezekiel 36:25-27; Joel 2:28; John 7:37-39. The power we receive is for the edification of the church and not for 'pride' or 'showing off.' (1Corinthians 12:7,12,13).

You are baptized with the Holy Ghost once. It is accompanied by the initial evidence of speaking a language previously unlearned, referred to as speaking in tongues as the Spirit gives utterance. (Acts 2:1- 8; 19:1-6.) Some denominations teach their congregation to speak in tongues. This becomes man made, therefore, there will be no power. This is why we have powerless Christians. The Holy Spirit can also be received by the laying of hands by a spirit filled man of God as in Acts 19:6. I will rather you pray earnestly to be baptized by Jesus and Jesus alone as in Acts 2:3-4 and Acts 10:44. There are many false religious leaders in this end time. Be careful who lays his hands on you.

Once you are baptized with the Holy Spirit, you are encouraged to pray for the refilling of the Spirit. This is referred to as the anointing of the Holy Spirit. After God has used you to do exploits, you need to pray for the refilling of the Spirit's power.

In the book of Luke, Jesus healed the woman with the issue of blood when she touched His garment in the midst of the crowd. In Luke 8:46 Jesus said, "Somebody hath touched me: for I perceive that virtue is gone out of me." (KJV)

When God assigns any work to you, He gives you the anointing to do it well, if you ask Him.(Luke 11:13).
This Holy Spirit baptism is for power to witness. "But ye shall receive power. After that the Holy Ghost is come upon you: and ye shall be witnesses unto Me both in Jerusalem, and in all Judea, and in Samaria, and unto the uttermost part of the earth." (Acts1:8 KJV).

How to receive the baptism of the Holy Spirit.
In Chapter 5, the word 'baptism' was explained as "to dip or immerse." You must desire to be dipped into or immersed into the Holy Spirit. Jesus Christ is the Baptizer. (Matt. 3:11; Mark 1:8; Luke 3:16; John 1:33).

To be baptized by Jesus you must:
(a). Thirst for it: have a strong desire to receive the anointing. (Isaiah 44:3; John 7:37,39; Psalm 42:1-2, 63:1-8). In the book of Acts, the disciples waited for this power with great expectation. They had enough time to settle their differences, hence the Bible records that they were in one accord on the day of Pentecost. While we wait and thirst, we should make sure that nothing will hinder this power from on high.

(b). Have faith that God will do what He has promised: Mark 11: 22, 24; Galatians 3:2, 14.

(c). Pray to receive the Holy Spirit. (Luke 11:13; Matt. 6: 8b).

Some benefits of the Holy Spirit baptism:
1. He empowers you to be a bold witness of the gospel. (Acts 1:8)
2. He fills you with joy, peace and boldness. (Acts 13:49-52)
3. He reveals the deep things of God. (1 Corinthians 2: 9-12)
4. He illuminates and inspires the word. (2 Peter 1:21)
5. He makes your praying effective. (Romans 8:26; James 5:16b)
6. He makes the Bible real to you as He guides you into all truth. (John 16:13).
7. He equips you with spiritual gifts to do exploits in the church of God; the body of Christ. (1 Corinthians 12:8 -11).

The nine gifts of the Holy Spirit to the body of Christ. Some believers receive more than one gift and some do not.
1. **"The word of Wisdom:** This is a wise utterance spoken through the operation of the Holy Spirit. It applies the revelation of God's word to a specific situation or problem. (Acts 6:10).
2. **Word of Knowledge:** This is an utterance inspired by the Holy Spirit that reveals knowledge about people, circumstances or Biblical truth. It is often connected with prophecy. (Acts 5:1-10).
3. **Faith:** This is a special supernatural faith imparted by the Holy Spirit that enables the Christian to believe God for the extraordinary and miraculous. It is the kind of faith that moves mountains. (Luke 17:6). This kind of faith is often found in combination with other manifestations.
4. **Gifts of Healing:** These gifts are given to the church to restore physical health by supernatural means. Gifts of healing means there are various kinds of illnesses in the church.

5. **Miraculous powers:** These are deeds of supernatural power that alter the normal course of nature. They include divine acts in which God's Kingdom is manifested against Satan and evil spirits.

6. **Prophecy:** We must distinguish between prophecy as a temporary manifestation of the Spirit and prophecy as a ministry gift of the church. (Ephesians 4:11).

7. **Discerning of spirits:** This gift is a special Spirit-given ability to properly discern evil spirits and to distinguish whether or not an utterance is from the Holy Spirit. (1 Corinthians 14:29, 1 John 4:1).

8. **Speaking in different kinds of tongues/ languages:** This involves the human spirit and the Spirit of God intermingling so that the believer communicates directly to God, (in prayer, praise, blessing and thanksgiving)." (Life in the Spirit Study Bible).

Many churches today are like the church in Corinth in regard to speaking in tongues. The Corinthians in Paul's days laid more emphasis on the gift of speaking in tongues and thereby neglected the other gifts. They deceived themselves by thinking that speaking in tongues was a show of spirituality. In some of our churches today, the members do the same thing. Some members who are not baptized in the Holy Spirit join them to utter any word that come to their minds. Some say what they hear their pastors say. They turn the church of God into a mad house. What a shame!!! Thank God that Apostle Paul corrected the Corinthians (1 Corinthians14). All ministers of the Word should study 1 Corinthians 14 and abide by the instructions given. Paul spoke in tongues more than all his members but he taught his congregation in the language they understood. His listeners were edified. (1Corinthians 14: 15–19, 32-33).

9. **Interpretation of tongues:** This gift may be given to anyone who is baptized in the Holy Spirit. In 1 Corinthians 14:28, Paul says "but if there is no interpreter, let him keep silence in the church; and let him speak to himself, and to God." The place for power is in your closet.

The Holy Spirit baptism is for all who meet God's conditions. "But you shall receive power, after that the Holy Ghost is come upon you: and ye shall be witnesses unto Me both in Jerusalem, and in all Judea, and in Samaria and unto the uttermost part of the earth." (Acts 1:8 KJV).

The Spirit also gives the church Apostles, Prophets, Evangelists, Pastors, Teachers, Deacons and helpers. These all work together to edify the church of the living God.

CHAPTER 9

SPREAD THE GOOD NEWS

When you receive Christ into your life, you become a new creature. You are born again. Your name is written in the book of life. All heaven bound passengers are mandated to tell others about their experience, the big change in their lives. When you buy a new car, or pass an examination or receive a present you have always longed to have, you are so happy and want to tell your family and friends about the exciting news. Receiving Christ as your Lord and Savior is good news. Sharing this good news is called "evangelism."

What is the Gospel?
The Greek word "evangelion" is translated as "gospel" or "good news." The good news or the gospel is that we who were hell bound are now set free through the death and resurrection of Christ. We can become heaven bound if we repent of our sins and believe in the Lord Jesus Christ. John 3:16–17 says "For God so loved the world that He gave His only begotten Son, that whoever believes in Him should not perish but have everlasting life. For God did not send His Son into the world to condemn the world but that the world through Him might be saved." (NKJV) God in His love, mercy and compassion brought us out of the darkness of the world into His marvelous light.

We need to tell others about this, with the aim of winning them to Christ if they are yet to be saved. The ministry of evangelism is for every believer and it starts from the day you become a believer in Christ. (Matt. 28:19–20; Mark 16:15; Acts 1:8). As a new convert, endeavor to read the Bible daily. Study the word.

2 Timothy 2:15 says "Study to show thyself approved unto God, a workman that needs not be ashamed, rightly dividing the word of truth." Reading the whole Bible in one year is another way of equipping yourself for personal evangelism.

Why is personal evangelism important?
Proverbs 11:30 says "The fruit of the righteous is a tree of life; and he that wins souls is wise." The primary purpose of our salvation is to win souls. (John 15:16). All Christians are chosen 'out of the world' (John 15:19) to 'bear fruit.' (John 15:2,4-5, 8). Fruit bearing refers to virtues, such as the fruit of the Spirit mentioned in chapter two as well as winning souls. Bringing others to saving faith in Christ has eternal reward. (Daniel 12:3; John 4:36; 12:24)

Most importantly, personal evangelism is essential and mandatory because:
(1). Jesus commanded it and practiced it: Matt. 28:19–20; Mark 16:15; Luke 15:10.
(2). Jesus wants His disciples to become 'fishers of men' and the Holy Spirit was given to help in soul winning. Matt. 4:19; Acts 1: 8.
(3). God does not want anyone to die in his sin: Ezekiel 33:11; 2 Peter 3:9.
(4) The early Christians practiced it. Acts 8:30–38. Believers are the light and salt of the world. They are the epistles which men read. It is important then that our lives should point others to Christ. "You are our epistle written in our hearts, known and read by all men; clearly you are an epistle of Christ, ministered by us, written not with ink but by the Spirit of the Living God; not on tablets of stone but on tablets of flesh, that is, of the heart." (2 Corinthians 3:2- 3).

Who is qualified to evangelize?

(a). You cannot give what you do not have. You must be sure that you are saved from sin before you can tell others about being saved. (2 Timothy 2:19-21).

(b). Live a holy life that people around you can testify to. (2 Timothy 2:4; Isaiah 52:11).

(c). You must be strongly convinced. In 1 Corinthians 9:16, Paul says, "For though I preach the gospel, I have nothing to glory of: for necessity is laid upon me; yea, woe is unto me, if I preach not the gospel!" (KJV). Such strong conviction will encourage you to put in everything to see a soul come to our Lord. No amount of strength, time or money will be counted as lost if we use it to usher in a soul into the Kingdom of God.

(d). Faith to believe that the Holy Spirit will speak through you to accomplish this ministry of reconciliation which is given to every believer. (2 Corinthians 5:19-20).

(e). Telling others about Jesus Christ is a debt we owe. (Romans 1:4; Ezekiel 33:6-7; Proverbs 24:11-12; 1 Corinthians 9:16; 1 John 3:16).

How do I start evangelizing since I do not know many Bible verses as my leader knows?

1. Your salvation testimony is a very good way to start: Your family and friends know about your old life. They have seen the big change in your behavior, tell them how it happened. What message from the Bible changed your life? Was it the life of a 'born again' Christian? Talk about the peace and joy that you now experience. Remember that your goal is to make him/her want to experience that joy and comfort. Always tell your listeners that you still experience challenges but you no longer worry about them because God knows and cares about them. God will perfect all that concerns you.

2. Friendship evangelism: Apostle Paul said that he became as weak to win the weak and became as poor to win the poor. (1 Corinthians 9:22). Jesus ate with sinners. (Luke 15:2). You should do all you can to get a sinner interested in the gospel message. (Giving good counsel, deeds of kindness, mowing the yard, taking in the trash cans, you can give out tracts or magazines).

3. Use the Romans road method: You can get all the scriptures for your outreach from the book of Romans. As you grow in faith and in the knowledge of the word, you will find that there are numerous verses of scripture that are relevant for soul-winning.

ROMANS ROAD TO SALVATION.

It is called the 'Romans road' because all the scriptures are from the book of Romans.

1. Recognize that you are a sinner. (Romans 3:23; 3:10-18).
2. The punishment for our sin is eternal death. (Romans 6:23).
3. Jesus paid the price for our sins while we were still sinners. He died to pay that debt. His resurrection from the dead shows that

God accepted that death as payment for our sins. (Romans 5:8-10)
4. All you need to do is (a) Believe that Jesus died for your sins. (b) Confess that Jesus is Lord. He has the final say in your life. He has power and authority over you. (c) Believe that He died and rose from the dead. (Christ's bodily death and resurrection is the central event in salvation). (Romans 10:9-10).
5. Forgiveness is available to anyone who will trust in Jesus as his Lord and Savior. (Romans 10:13).

Some benefits of being saved (Excerpts from the book of Romans):
Romans 5:1: You are justified and you have peace with God.
Romans 8:1: There is no more condemnation for those who are in Christ.
Romans 8: 38-39: Nothing can separate you from the love of God if you hold steadfastly to your confession.
Romans 8:16: The Spirit bears witness that you are a child of God.
Romans 10:17: You grow in faith as you hear and read the word of God.
Romans 8:11: The Spirit that raised up Jesus, will heal you.

Conclusion:
God blesses every believer; we should share the blessings. The woman in John 4:28, left her water pot to go and share the good news. Personal evangelism is urgent for we do not know when the Lord shall come. Just as there is reward for winning souls, there is judgment for not warning sinners. (Ezekiel 3:19-20). Sow the seed and our God will water it. Remember the person you want to win to Jesus, in your daily prayer. May God richly bless you as you obey His command. He died that we may live.

CHAPTER 10

FORGIVENESS IS IMPORTANT FOR OUR HEAVENLY JOURNEY

God, the Creator of Heaven and earth forgives us when we repent of our evil deeds and ask for forgiveness. Man, God's creature, finds it difficult to forgive even when the offender repents and asks for forgiveness. "The heart is deceitful above all things, and desperately wicked: who can know it?" asks Prophet Jeremiah. (Jeremiah 17:9). Genesis 6: 5-7 says, "Then the Lord saw that the wickedness of man was great in the earth, and that every intent of the thoughts of his heart was only evil continually. And the Lord was sorry that He had made man on the earth, and He was grieved in His heart. So, the Lord said, "I will destroy man whom I have created from the face of the earth, both man and beast, creeping things and birds of the air, for I am sorry that I have made them." God was happy when He, the Son and the Holy Spirit created man. Genesis 1:26 "And God said, Let Us make man in Our image, after Our likeness: and let them have dominion over the fish of the sea, and over the fowl of the air, and over the cattle, and over all the earth, and over every creeping thing that creeps on the earth." God made provision for man's happiness but man chose to disobey and annoy God. Thank God for Noah, who in the midst of all the wicked men chose to please God. Genesis 6:8 says, "But Noah found grace in the eyes of the Lord." We need many people like Noah today so we can be sure of making heaven our final abode. We all know the story of the end of that wicked generation. God used Noah to witness to them but they did not repent. Noah was building the Ark as a place of refuge but the people were not bothered. (Luke 17:27; Matt. 24:38).

"They ate, they drank, they married wives, they were given in marriage, until the day Noah entered the ark, and the flood came and destroyed them all. Only Noah and his family who were in the Ark were saved." God destroyed them with the flood and started another generation with Noah.

One would have thought that the generation started by Noah, the righteous man, would have been a righteous nation. Man, still remained wicked. Unforgiveness, greed, jealousy, pride and many wicked deeds still found a place in the heart of man. They had the same privilege as the world before theirs, but they did not appreciate God's love and kindness. God's eyes are too pure to behold sin, so He decided to accept the blood of animals to atone for our sins.

Instead of obeying God and fleeing from sin, some worshiped those animals and others carved objects and worshiped them as their creator. God hates idolatry. He does not share His glory with anyone. God was angry with man but had to try another plan.

The Bible says in Galatians 4: 4-5, "But when the fullness of the time was come, God sent His Son, made of a woman, made under the law, to redeem them that are under the law, that we might receive the adoption as sons." Jesus is the Son sent by God. He is the only mediator between God and man. He came to save the world from their sins and reconcile us with God. As many as receive Him, He gives power to become the sons of God. When you are a child of God you have the right to call God, 'Abba Father.'

Jesus fulfilled His assignment in the world, through teaching, preaching, healing the sick and casting out demons. He was very concerned about our relationship with God and other people around us, especially with His followers. In Matt. 18:15 -17, Jesus teaches us how believers should settle their conflicts.

Step 1. Go and tell your brother his fault in private. If he listens and pays attention, you have won back your brother.

Step 2. If he does not listen, take along with you one or two witnesses. The principle of witnesses is taken from Deut.19:15. The one or two believers are to witness that; the offended brother is acting in good faith and is working towards reconciliation. They will also be witnesses to any agreement.

Step 3. If he does not pay attention to them, then tell it to the church.

Step 4. If he does not listen to the church, then treat him as an unbeliever. The question then, is how do you treat an unbeliever? Every unbeliever needs to know Jesus and receive Him as his Lord and Savior. Pray for his salvation. When he is saved, he will understand that "love" bears all things and believes all things. The truth is that, if we follow the counsel of Jesus, most conflicts could be resolved. At every step let restoration be the goal and not casting blame.

How many times must we forgive our brother?
The tradition of the rabbis was that you can only forgive your brother three times for the same offence. When Peter asked Jesus in Matt. 18:21, "Lord, how many times will my brother sin against me and I forgive him and let it go? Up to seven times?" Peter was being generous and expected the Lord to appreciate his suggestion. I believe that many of us will give Peter a pass mark. Jesus answered him in verse 22 "I say to you, not up to seven times, but seventy times seven." Are these four hundred and ninety times in a day for

the same offense or other offenses as well? In whichever way you look at it, Jesus is teaching us to cultivate a spirit of forgiveness and not the habit of counting offenses. Jesus now backs up His answer with the parable that shows how God views the sin of unforgiveness. A parable is an earthly illustration that has a heavenly meaning.

Matt. 18:23-35 reads,
(v23) Therefore the Kingdom of heaven is like a king who wished to settle accounts with his slaves.
(24) When he began the accounting, one who owed him 10,000 talents was brought to him.
(25) But because he could not repay, his master ordered him to be sold, with his wife and his children and everything that he possessed, and payment to be made.
(26) So, the slave fell on his knees and begged him, saying, "Have patience with me and I will repay you everything."
(27) And his master's heart was moved with compassion and he released him and forgave him(cancelling) the debt.
(28) But that same slave went out and found one of his fellow slaves who owed him a hundred denarii; and he seized him and began choking him, saying, "pay what you owe!"
(29) So, his fellow slave fell on his knees and begged him earnestly, "Have patience with me and I will repay you."
(30) But he was unwilling and he went and had him thrown in prison until he paid back the debt.
(31) When his fellow slaves saw what had happened, they were deeply grieved and they went and reported to their master (with clarity and in detail) everything that had taken place.
(32) Then his master called him and said to him, "You wicked and contemptible slave, I forgave all that (great) debt of yours because you begged me.

(33) Should you not have had mercy on your fellow slave (who owed you little by comparison), as I had mercy on you?"
(34) And in wrath his master turned him over to the torturers (jailers) until he paid all that he owed.
(35) My heavenly Father will also do the same to (every one of) you, if each of you does not forgive his brother from your heart." (Amplified Study Bible).
In this parable, the King symbolizes God and to settle accounts symbolizes divine judgment. The first slave owed the King 10,000 talents. "1 talent would be worth about 6,000 days' work, so it would take over 190,000 years for someone to pay off a debt of 10,000 talents." (Jeremiah Study Bible). The King had ordered that he, his wife and children and all that he possessed be sold to repay the debt. The proceeds from that sale would not even repay the amount he owed. God in His mercy and compassion, forgave him and cancelled his debt when he asked for pardon. A 100 denarii was equivalent to 90 days of wages. The second slave was more honest when he promised his fellow slave that he will repay the debt. His debt was small and manageable.

The contrast between the 10,000 talents and the 100 denarii shows that the sins of others against us are trivial in comparison to the enormity of our own sins against God. "In this parable, Jesus teaches that the forgiveness of God, though freely given to repentant sinners, nevertheless remains conditional, according to a person's willingness to forgive others. In other words, if we are not merciful and are unforgiving toward another person, that will block the flow of God's forgiveness toward us." (Life in the Spirit Study Bible). (Matt. 6:14-15; Ephesians 4:31-32; Hebrews 12:15). The debtor's torture will continue until the debt is paid in full. Since the debt could not possibly be repaid, the torture symbolizes eternal punishment in hell.

Conclusion:
One of the first scriptures most believers memorize is in Matt. 6: 9-15. This is commonly referred to as the Lord's Prayer. It is recited at home and in most churches. If only Christians will meditate on what they recite and do it, this world will be a better place to live in. In reciting or praying the 'Lord's Prayer,' believers ignorantly or intentionally ignore verses 14 and 15 of Matt.6. "For if we forgive men their trespasses, your heavenly Father will also forgive you: But if you forgive not men their trespasses, neither will your Father forgive your trespasses." Furthermore, remember that unforgiveness may lead to hatred. Christians treat this sin of unforgiveness with levity but God is serious with His pronouncement. In 1John 3:15, the Bible says, "Whoever hates his brother is a murderer, and you know that no murderer has eternal life abiding in him." (NKJV).

God is grieved to see His children perish in hell for the sin they could have avoided. His grace is sufficient for us. Come out of that pride and forgive. Jesus has paid the price already. Speaking from my personal experience, if you forgive your offender, (no matter the gravity of the offence) the Lord fills your heart with indescribable joy and peace. You will not want to lose that joy. You will go the extra mile, asking for forgiveness even when you are right. May God open your eyes to see the need to forgive all who have offended you. There are people you have wronged. Today is the day to reconcile and make peace with all men. (Matt. 5: 22-24). Ezekiel cried, "Why will you die, O house of Israel?" I cry, "Why will you perish, O beloved children of God?

CHAPTER 11

GIVE GOD HIS RIGHTFUL PLACE

God created man for His glory and expects man to declare His praise. Many people only praise God when things are going well for them. When things seem not to favor them, they blame God. If we truly know the God we serve, we will have no choice but to worship and praise Him in our good and bad days. "Let everything that has breath praise the Lord." (Psalm 150:6). The Psalmist lists a few reasons why man should praise God in Psalm 146. **(5)** "Happy is he who has the God of Jacob for his help, whose hope is in the Lord his God, **(6)** Who made heaven and earth, the sea and all that are in them, who keeps truth forever, **(7)** Who executes justice for the oppressed; who gives food to the hungry. The Lord gives freedom to the prisoners. **(8)** The Lord opens the eyes of the blind; the Lord raises those who are bowed down. The Lord loves the righteous. **(9)**. The Lord watches over the strangers; He relieves the fatherless and widows; but the way of the wicked He turns upside down." If you will count your blessings one by one, you will find that God has blessed you in every area of your life. A songwriter, W. Spencer Walton, sums up his praise for God thus "while with adoring wonder His blessings I retrace. It seems as if eternal days are far too short to sound His praise." Our God is good to all who are willing to obey Him.

True worship and praise should come from our hearts. "God is Spirit, and those who worship Him must worship Him in spirit and truth." (John 4:24). You need the second birth, (birth of the Spirit) to worship God acceptably. Man is created to worship God, his creator.

The Israelites worshiped God as long as Moses was with them. When God called Moses to Mount Sinai to give him the Ten Commandments, the people worshiped the 'golden calf' which Aaron made. (Exodus 32:1-9). Consequently, God was angry with His children and said to Moses in Exodus 32:10, "Now therefore, let me alone, that my wrath may burn hot against them and I may consume them. And I will make of you a great nation." Moses rejected that offer but pleaded for forgiveness for his brethren. There is always punishment for sin if there is no repentance. Only the sons of Levi repented. Moses said to them (the sons of Levi) in Exodus 32:27-28 "Thus says the Lord God of Israel: Let every man put his sword on his side, and go in and out from entrance to entrance throughout the camp, and let every man kill his brother, every man his companion and every man his neighbor." So, the sons of Levi did according to the word of Moses. And about three thousand men of the people fell that day." Read Exodus 32 to understand the wrath of God. God has not changed. He will pour out His wrath on anyone who worships any other 'god.'

God is angry when we give first place to His creatures:

When the Israelites were rescued from Pharaoh of Egypt, the Lord told Moses that He would visit them in the wilderness of Sinai. They were to sanctify themselves for three days before the Lord would come to meet them. "So, Moses went down from the mountain to the people and sanctified the people, and they washed their clothes. And he said to the people, "Be ready for the third day; do not come near your wives." (Exodus 19:14-15). Read Exodus chapters 19 and 20 to learn more about the Lord's visit to His children in the wilderness of Sinai.

God visited them in the midst of the fire. Moses set bounds around the mountain so the people could not trespass. In the book of Deuteronomy, Moses explained that God spoke to them from the fire so that no one will make images of Him and worship it. "Take careful heed to yourselves, for you saw no form when the Lord spoke to you at Horeb out of the midst of the fire, lest you act corruptly and make for yourselves a carved image in the form of any figure: the likeness of male or female, the likeness of any animal that is on the earth or the likeness of any winged bird that flies in the air, the likeness of anything that creeps on the ground or the likeness of any fish that is in the water beneath the earth. And take heed, lest you lift your eyes to heaven, and when you see the sun, the moon, and the stars, all the host of heaven, you feel driven to worship them and serve them, which the Lord your God has given to all the peoples under the whole heaven as a heritage." (Deut. 4:15-19).

Our God is awesome. He is a great God. No human can make any image which can represent God. No one knows what He looks like. He revealed Himself to the Israelites in the midst of fire. Those who make images of God with wood, precious stones, and many of the things which God created are dishonoring God. They have not seen God. They are belittling God.

The worst is to bow before those images and worship them. Isaiah 42:8 says, "I am the Lord, that is My name; And My glory I will not give to another; Nor My praise to carved images." Our God is a jealous God and will not share His glory with His creature. Isaiah 44:9 reads, "Those who make an image, all of them are useless, and their precious things shall not profit; They are their own witnesses; They neither see nor know that they may be ashamed." I sometimes wonder if those who worship idols and different images have ever considered what the Psalmist observed about idols in Psalm 115 verses 4-8? "Their idols are silver and gold, the work of men's hands.

They have mouths but they do not speak; Eyes they have but they do not see; They have ears but they do not hear; Noses they have, but they do not smell; They have hands but they do not handle; Feet they have, but they do not walk; Nor do they mutter through their throat. Those who make them are like them; so is everyone who trusts in them." If there is bad weather and you have to evacuate, your 'mini god' has to be carried. It cannot help you. Is that not a burden to you?

In Judges 6, God told Gideon to tear down the altar of Baal which his father, Joash worshiped and cut down the wooden image beside the altar. Gideon obeyed God. "Then the men of the city said to Joash, "Bring your son, that he may die, because he had cut down the wooden image that was beside it." But Joash said to all who stood against him, "Would you plead for Baal? Would you save him? Let the one who would plead for him be put to death in the morning! If he is a god, let him plead for himself, because his altar has been torn down." (Judges 6:30-31). Joash understood that 'idols' are helpless. You should do the same.

What is an 'Idol?'

An idol is anything you love more than God. Anything you give a place above God in your life. An idol is anything you devote your time and energy to and will ignore other people and even God to fulfill that desire. Do Christians worship idols? Many Christians ignorantly make idols and worship them. Isaiah 40:18 asks this question. "To whom then will you liken God? Or what likeness will you compare to Him?" No image or picture can represent the personality of God. God's supremacy in all areas cannot be bottled into an image or picture. God is holy and His understanding is unsearchable. Some believe that the images or pictures of God help them think of God and His wonderful works. You are wrong my brothers and sisters.

A Christian's concept of God must be based on the revealed word of God, the Bible. Jesus came and revealed God to us. All we need to know about God's power, goodness, mercy and love are in His holy Word. You have experienced God's wonderful blessings in your life. God is not done with you. You are blessed every day. That you are alive today is one of God's mercies. You do not need an image or picture to remind you of God. He is your 'Emmanuel.' (God with us'). If you continue to use the images or pictures in your place of worship, you are an idolater. Apostle John in 1John 5:21 says, "Little children, keep yourselves from idols. Amen." He knew that in our struggles in life, we will face the difficulties of being able to continually keep God first in our lives.

Our idols in this present age, may be loved ones, material possessions, recognition, money or education. The emphasis is not to give them preeminence in your life. God should always be first. Nothing should compete with God. (Matt. 19:29; Mark 10:17-30; Luke 18:29 - 30). Matt. 10:37 says, "He who loves father or mother more than Me is not worthy of Me; and he who loves son or daughter more than Me is not worthy of Me." Luke 14:26 also says, "If anyone comes to Me and does not hate his father and mother, wife and children, brothers and sisters, yes, and even his own life also, he cannot be My disciple." To hate your loved ones as quoted in Luke, means to "love them less." Jesus wants us to love our families but we should ensure that God reigns supreme in our lives. Christ demands that our commitment to and love for Him should be greater than the love for any person or thing. "Then He said to another, "Follow me." But he said, "Lord, let me first go and bury my father." Jesus said to him, "Let the dead bury their own dead but you go and preach the Kingdom of God." (Luke 9:59-60).It is wrong for a Christian to stop going to worship God in church or stop attending prayer meetings because he lost a loved one.

Read the answer Jesus gave to the man in Luke 9:60. If you continue to do the work of the Kingdom despite your loss or challenges, you are putting God first in your life.

It is great to be rich if you acknowledge that your riches come from God. (Deut. 8:18). The Bible says it all. "For the love of money is a root of all kinds of evil, for which some have strayed from the faith in their greediness, and pierced themselves through with many sorrows." (1Timothy 6:10). Money should not be our waking thought. Covetousness and greed are grouped as idolatry because one's focus on material things and desires do not give God the first place. (Colossians 3:5) Always put God first because He made you rich. You may be rich today and poor tomorrow. God has many poor and needy people in the world. The rich should help them.

Conclusion:
God is our creator. He does not want us to make his creatures our gods. God is a Spirit so we must worship Him in spirit and in truth. Let us endeavor to put God first in all we do and say. Matt. 6:33 says; "But seek first the kingdom of God and His righteousness, and all these things shall be added to you." God is faithful. He will always keep His promise. Let us bless our God at all times and let His praise continually be in our mouths. Amen. God has instructions for the 'Rich.' "Command those who are rich in this present age not to be haughty, nor to trust in uncertain riches but in the living God, who gives us richly all things to enjoy. Let them do good, that they be rich in good works, ready to give, willing to share, storing up for themselves a good foundation for the time to come, that they may lay hold on eternal life." (1Tim. 6:17-19). We now know the will of God about giving Him the first place in our lives. His grace is sufficient for us. Let us ask and He will give us the divine enablement to obey. Our God answers prayers.

CHAPTER 12

CHARITABLE DEEDS, PRAYER AND FASTING ARE ESSENTIAL FOR THIS JOURNEY

Jesus is the epitome of kindness. The Bible says that He went about doing good. I pray that He will visit every one of us today. In Matt. 6:2,3,5,6, Jesus used the word 'when' you do good deeds, pray or fast. He assumed that His disciples would regularly assist needy people. I understand that the temple in Jesus' days had about 13 trumpet-shaped openings into which people placed their financial contributions. Hypocrites often converted their gifts into the largest number of coins possible so their money would make a loud noise when dropped into the trumpet-shaped opening. Jesus' teaching on 'alms giving' or 'charitable deeds' emphasizes the fact that, not all good deeds please the Lord.

The deeds that get heaven's attention:
Deut. 15:7-11; Matt. 6:1–7, 16-18; 25:35–46; 1 John 3:17-18.
Jesus encouraged believers to help the less privileged, the church and other organizations that work to improve our standard of living. He also emphasized that the poor will always be in our midst. In James 1:27, the Bible teaches, "that pure and undefiled religion before God and the Father is, to visit orphans and widows in their trouble, and to keep ourselves unspotted from the world." Isaiah 1:17 says, "Learn to do good; seek justice; rebuke the oppressor; defend the fatherless, plead for the widow." When we give alms, we are indirectly giving it to God. (Deut. 8:18) "And you shall remember the Lord your God, for it is He who gives you power to get wealth." Matt. 25:35-46, reminds us that whatever we do to any of God's creatures, we do it to Him.

Knowing that God, to whom we give gifts knows our motives, we should not do good or give gifts for the admiration of others. Some do good for selfish reasons. If our giving does not glorify God, we will lose our reward from God. We would be like hypocrites who pretend to give God glory but seek to glorify themselves. Jesus' condemnation of doing acts of righteousness to be seen by others is a warning to those who advertise their success, who want to be recognized by their 'titles' and who want to have the first place in every gathering. Any charitable deed that is done to please man and not God, is an abomination to God. It is not recognized in heaven. (Matt. 6:1-4). Give in secret and God will reward you openly.

What the Bible teaches about fasting:
Joshua 7:6-11; 2 Chronicles 20:1-27; Ezra 8:21-23; Nehemiah 1:2-4; Esther 4:1-3,15,16; Isaiah 58:3-14; Joel 2:12-27; Daniel 9: 3, 10:3; Matt. 6:16-18.
Fasting is a biblical way to truly be humble in the sight of God. A brother describes scriptural fasting as a continuous prayer without words. Fasting is the discipline of abstaining from food or any kind of pleasure for spiritual purposes. Jesus fasted while He was on earth and expects His disciples to do the same. In Matt. 9:15, Jesus said "that the days will come when the bridegroom shall be taken from them, and then shall they fast." The Church is waiting for the return of the Bridegroom, (Matt.25:6; John 14:3). Therefore, fasting at this time is **(a)** a sign of the believer's longing for the Lord's return, **(b)** a way to increase spiritual intimacy with Christ, **(c)** a placing of the interest of His Kingdom above our own, **(d)** a heart preparation for the end of age and Christ's coming, **(e)** a mourning of Christ's absence, **(f)** a sign of sorrow for the sins of the world, and **(g)** a time of intercession for the unsaved.

There are different ways of fasting **(1)** Abstaining from all food, solid or liquid **(2)** Abstaining from both food and water (Esther 4:16; Acts 9:9) The body needs water so abstaining from liquid should not be for more than three days because the kidney may begin to shut down and the body will dehydrate. **(3)** A restriction of diet. (Daniel 10:3) No one should go on protracted fasting except directed by God. Moses and Elijah fasted 40 days and 40 nights without food or water but that was under supernatural condition. (Exodus 24:18; Deut. 9:9,18; 1 Kings 19:8) As you grow older and are on many medications you may have to consult your doctor before going on absolute fast. Always bear in mind that it is not your fasting that touches the heart of God but your heart. God in His mercy will grant your request according to His will. Psalm 115:3 says, that our God is in Heaven and does whatever He pleases. Isaiah 40:28 says that God's understanding is unsearchable. Fast with a clean heart and a good motive and wait for the Almighty God to move in your favor.

Conditions for a genuine Prayer and Fasting.
Many people pray and fast but do not get answers to their prayers. You do not just wake up one morning and decide to pray and fast. You are dealing with God and not man. Our God needs to be feared and reverenced. Sin causes a separation between us and God. Let us depart from iniquity and draw near to God. There must be a purpose for fasting. You must have a reason for waiting on the Lord.

(1) Is it for more anointing for the task ahead? **(2)** Is it to mourn for personal sin and failure? **(3)** Is it to mourn over the sins of the church, nation or the world? **(4)** Is it for good health for you and your family? **(5)** Is it for spiritual growth? **(6)** For divine intervention in respect of court cases, examinations or interviews? **(7)** Is it against opposing spiritual forces? **(8)** Is it for traveling mercies? **(9)** Is it for the barren? **(10)** Is it for the pregnant?

(11) Is it for the salvation of your family? **(12)** Is it for the Global Pandemic to cease? **(13)** Is it to gain revelation and wisdom concerning God's will? **(14)** Is it for revival while we wait for the Lord's return? **(15)** Is it for God's provision and protection? **(16)** Is it for a spouse? **(17)** Is it for lifting of any type of burden? Whatever you are praying for is already known by our God who is able to make impossible things possible. He says "unto me shall all flesh come."

Deciding to fast and pray involves: **(1)** A heavy burden in your heart or yoke which only God can break. You are helpless and you are convinced that no man can help you. **(2) Humility**: You must be humble before God because God gives grace to the humble and despises the proud. No matter your wealth or education, God is no respecter of persons. **(3) Faith**: Your faith can move mountains. You must trust God for the answer to your prayer. Hebrews 11:6 says "But without faith it is impossible to please Him, for He who comes to God must believe that He is, and that He is a rewarder of those who diligently seek Him." (NKJV). If you allow doubt or confusion to override your faith, your fasting is in vain. Do not allow the enemy to cheat you. 'Trust in the Lord and take heart,' says the Hymn writer. "Behold, I am the Lord, the God of all flesh. Is there anything too hard for Me?" (Jeremiah. 32:27 NKJV). Our God will take away our heavy burdens and set us free in Jesus name. Amen. **(4) Obedience**: We must be willing to obey God's word and also listen attentively to the leading of the Spirit. God may reveal to you what you are not doing right. "For whom the Lord loves He corrects, just as a father, the son in whom He delights." (Proverbs 3:12 NKJV). **(5) Unity**: Clear all malice and animosity. Settle all disputes and be at peace with everyone; (husband, wife, children or neighbors). Matt.5:23-24 says, "Therefore if you bring your gift to the altar, and there remember that your brother has something against you, leave your gift there before the altar, and go your way. First be reconciled to your brother and then come and offer your gift." (NKJV).

In 2 Chronicles 20:13, King Jehoshaphat and all Judah stood before the Lord, with their little ones, wives and children, (unity). In Joel 2: 16-17, they all gathered in one accord to fast and pray. In Esther chapter 4, Queen Esther, Mordecai and all the Jews were in unity to wait on the Lord. When we have met these conditions, we are assured that God will hear our prayers and answer us at His own time.

How to spend time before God during fasting:
1. Search the scriptures to have relevant passages or promises of God on which you can stand when you pray.
2. Decide when to start and when to stop.
3. Be clean: Matt. 6:17-18a, "But you, when you fast, anoint your head and wash your face, so that you do not appear to men to be fasting, but to your Father who is in the secret place."
4. Start your prayers with praises, thanksgiving and confession of sins.
5. Use your hymn or chorus book.
6. Read your Bible, meditate on the word and pray. Table your request before God. Pour out your heart to God. He knows all about your problems but He wants you to say them. Mark.10:51-52.
7. Every hour, pray again reminding God of your requests. You can read other relevant scriptures and sing praises. If you are at work, "shooting prayers" like Nehemiah's will work. Nehemiah 2:4.
8.At the end of your fasting, you should pray and thank God for answered prayer. This is just a suggestion. Spend your period of "prayer and fasting" the best way you know.

Conclusion:
Jesus wants us to fast and pray as we wait for His return. (Matt. 9:15b). King David waited on the Lord anytime he had a burden (Psalm 25:3-5; 27:13-14; Luke 2:25, 36-38). Jesus taught His disciples that there are yokes which cannot be broken except through prayer and fasting. (Matt. 17:14-21; Mark 9:16-29). Jesus also spent nights in prayer. (Luke 6:12-13). Isaiah 40:31 says, "But those who wait on the Lord shall renew their strength; they shall mount up with wings like eagles, they shall run and not be weary, they shall walk and not faint." (NKJV).

Those who wait on the Lord are promised:
(1) The strength of God to revive them in the midst of exhaustion and weakness, of suffering and trials.
(2) The ability to rise above their difficulties like an eagle that soars into the sky.
(3) The ability to run spiritually without tiring and to walk steadily forward without fainting at God's delays.
God promises that if His people will patiently trust Him, He will provide whatever is needed to sustain them constantly.
Doing the will of God brings joy. The Kingdom of God is righteousness, peace and joy in the Holy Ghost. "Rejoice in the Lord always." (Philippians 4:4).

CHAPTER 13

THE LORD'S SUPPER

The Lord's Supper was the center of early Christian worship. They gathered around one table, with each other in unity. Christ had expressed this type of humility and unity when He instituted the Supper. (Matt. 26:26 - 30; Mark 14:22 -26; Luke 22:14-20).
Jesus declared "Do this in remembrance of Me." The Lord's Supper was instituted so that all believers might partake and remember the Lord's death until He comes. Christ's death is our ultimate motivation against falling into sin and for abstaining from all appearance of evil. (1 Thess. 5:22). It is a thanksgiving for the blessings and salvation of God made available by Christ's sacrifice on the cross. (Matt. 26:27; Mark 14:23; Luke 22:19; 1 Corinthians 11:24). We have fellowship with other believers and Jesus is the Host. (1 Corinthians 10:16-17; Matt. 18:20). It is a proclamation of the new covenant. We look forward to the rapture and marriage supper of the Lamb (Revelation 19:7-9).

The emblems are the "unleavened bread" and "the fruit of the vine." The unleavened bread represents the broken body of Christ while the fruit of the vine represents His shed blood. These are symbols. While we expect Him, we try to be like Jesus in kindness, helping the poor and needy, evangelizing, reading the word and doing it, praying for and with others. This institution of the Lord's Supper is clearly shown in the gospels. Apostle Paul amplified it in 1 Corinthians 11: 26.

The Feast of the Unleavened Bread also called the Passover: Exodus 12:1-51; Deut. 16:1-8.

We may all be familiar with the story of the Israelites in Egypt and how Pharaoh refused to let them go to worship Jehovah. God sent many plagues to convince Pharaoh that He is the Almighty God, but, because God had hardened the heart of Pharaoh, he did not let Moses and the children of Israel go. God finally used the death of every first born of all the Egyptians and the first born of all their animals to force Pharaoh to let the Israelites go. Exodus 12:1-51 has the entire story. In verse 7, God instructed Moses and the children of Israel to take some of the blood of the lamb and put it on the two door posts and on the lintel of their houses.

Exodus 12:12-14 says, "for I will pass through the land of Egypt on that night, and will strike all the firstborn in the land of Egypt, both man and beast; and against all the gods of Egypt I will execute judgment: I am the Lord. Now the blood shall be a sign for you on the houses where you are. And when I see the blood, I will pass over you; and the plague shall not be on you to destroy you when I strike the land of Egypt. So, this day shall be to you a memorial; and you shall keep it as a feast to the Lord throughout your generations. You shall keep it as a feast by an everlasting ordinance."

All Israelites observed this Passover feast in remembrance of how God saved them and their children but killed all the first born of the Egyptians. Jesus also kept this feast until the last night before He was arrested and crucified. Then He said to them, "With fervent desire I have desired to eat this Passover with you before I suffer;" (Luke 22:15. NKJV). The celebration of Passover was a holy gathering. All participants must be clean according to the law of Moses. They read the story about their deliverance from the book of Exodus. (Ex. 12:1-14).

They sang the Hallel Psalms 113 to 118 (Jewish Prayer of Praise). The dates for the Passover became the beginning of months for the Jews. The blood of an unblemished lamb and unleavened bread were used. The lamb was roasted and not eaten raw and no bone of the lamb should be broken. (Exodus 12:46; John 19:36) They concluded with prayers. The defiled, the uncircumcised strangers and the Gentiles did not participate. (Exodus 12 :43-49) The Jews looked forward to the Passover feast with excitement and great expectation. (2 Chronicles 30:17-27). Jesus and His disciples sang a hymn at the end of the feast in Matt. 26:30.

The Lord's Supper / the Passover:
1 Corinthians 5:7 -8; John 1:29, 36; Isaiah 53:7; 1Peter1:19.
The shedding of Christ's blood replaced the shedding of the blood of animals to atone for our sins. The Lord's Supper replaced the feast of the Passover. Jesus is called our Passover Lamb in 1 Corinthians 5:7. Jesus commands every believer to receive His body and blood (The unleavened bread and the "fruit of the vine") until He returns. It is compulsory for every leader of God's assembly or fellowship, to make adequate provision for the flock of God to obey our Lord in this area. Here, in America, almost all Christian bookshops stock the bread and wine for communion. We have no reason to disobey our Lord's command. "Do this in remembrance of Me." In some assemblies, the Lord's Supper is called "The Eucharist," "The Lord's table," or "The Holy Communion." Whatever name you choose to call it, the conditions for receiving it does not vary.

To receive the Lord's Supper: the communicant must be free from sin. (Confess your sins, make peace and restore what does not belong to you). Set your thoughts on what Christ accomplished for you and focus on His return. The Lord's Supper is for believers who are not defiled. Come in humble adoration.

It is a serious thing to come to the communion with an unprepared heart. It is also a serious thing to receive the supper in a careless manner. The Corinthians had been sinning in their observation of the Lord's Supper and God had to discipline them. "For this reason, many are weak and sickly among you, and many sleep (have died)" (1Corinthians 11:30).After you have received the Lord's Supper, spend some time to pray and thank God.

Conclusion:
Most of us try to forget how those we love died, but Jesus wants us to remember how He died. This is because everything we have as Christians centers on His death and resurrection. We also remember why He died: Christ died for our sins. He was our substitute, paying the debt we could not pay. (Isaiah 53:6; 1 Peter 2:24). We remember how He died willingly, meekly and showing His love for us. (Romans 5:8) He bore on His body the sins of the world. The most important thing is that we can reach out by faith and have fellowship with our Living Savior. 1 Corinthians 11:26 says, "For as often as you eat this bread and drink this cup, you proclaim the Lord's death till He comes." The return of Jesus is the blessed hope of the church and every believer. Jesus rose from the dead and ascended into Heaven. He shall return to take us to Heaven and we shall be like Him. (1 John 3:2).

The Lord's Supper is a family meal. Jesus wants us to love and care for one another. Can we remember the Lord's death and not love one another? "Beloved, if God so loved us, we also ought to love one another." (1 John 4:11 NKJV). Jesus did not specify how often we should receive the Lord's Supper so some churches celebrate it daily, some weekly, some monthly and others quarterly. Let us be obedient and observe this ordinance reverently as we wait for our coming King.

CHAPTER 14

THE RAPTURE AND THE GREAT TRIBULATION

The Rapture:
Matt. 24:36; Luke 21:34-36; John 14:1-3; Acts 1:9-11; 1 Corinthians 15:51-58; 1Thess. 4:13-18.

The word "rapture" is not used in the Bible but it has the literal meaning of "caught up." Jesus ascended into Heaven after His resurrection. His disciples watched Him until the clouds received Him out of their sight. Acts 1: 10-11 says, "And while they looked steadfastly toward Heaven as He went up, behold, two men stood by them in white apparel, who also said "Men of Galilee, why do you stand gazing up into heaven? This same Jesus, who was taken up from you into heaven, will so come in like manner as you saw Him go into heaven." God's word does not change; He will surely come in the clouds. 1Thess. 4:17 describes the rapture as the time when the saints on earth will be caught up together in the clouds with those who had died in Christ. They will meet the Lord in the air and will live with Him forever.

The rapture marks the end of the church age. Jesus will take the saints away before the Great Tribulation. God does not want His children to suffer with the world. God saved Noah and his family before He destroyed the world with flood. The angels were sent to take Lot and his family out of Sodom before God destroyed it with fire. God sheltered Jacob in the house of his uncle, Laban to escape the wrath of his brother Esau. God sheltered Moses in the desert for forty years to escape the wrath of his brethren and the Egyptians.

Three unique sounds will be involved in this event:
The Lord's shout, the sound of the trumpet, and the voice of the Archangel. In John 11:43, Jesus shouted outside the tomb of Lazarus and Lazarus rose from the dead. His shout at the rapture will raise the dead saints. Those in the graves will hear His voice. (John 5:28). The Jewish people were familiar with trumpets. Trumpets were used to declare war, to announce special times and seasons and to gather the people for a journey. (Numbers 10). The trumpet of God will sound just before the saints are caught up in the air. The angels will surely rejoice at Christ's victory. The voice of the Archangel is heard as the Lord waits for His own in the air.

These men were raptured: Genesis 5:24; 2 Kings 2:11-12.
The Old Testament saints Enoch and Elijah were translated in a moment of time and caught up in the air. For Enoch the Bible says that, "he was not; for God took him." The people in the days of Elijah went out searching for him but could not find him. Generations later, the Jews still believed that they will see Elijah return to this world. Jesus told His disciples that Elijah had come but they did not recognize him. He came in the spirit of John the Baptist. (Malachi 4: 5-6; Matt. 11:10-14; Luke 1: 17). At the transfiguration, Peter, James and John saw Elijah and Moses and were convinced that Elijah was in Heaven after he was raptured. These men walked with God and never gave up. God will give us the grace to watch and pray and be ready like Enoch and Elijah.

What will happen to the raptured saints?
The shout of Jesus will raise the dead in Christ. "In the twinkling of an eye," the living believers' bodies will be clothed with immortality. (1 Corinthians 15:51-53). All the saints will be caught up together to meet the Lord in the air.

They will be visibly united with Christ; they will be united with their loved ones who had died in Christ. Jesus will take them to His Father's house. (1 Thess. 4:13-18; John 14:2-3). He will not be visible to the unrepentant in the world.

Saints will be removed from all distress, oppression, sin and death. (Philippians 3:21; 1 Corinthians 15:51-52). 1 Thess. 1:10 says ,"And to wait for His Son from Heaven, whom He raised from the dead, even Jesus who delivers us from the wrath to come." (The great Tribulation).

Immediately after the Rapture, the saints in Heaven will face the judgment seat of Christ. (1 Corinthians 3:11-15). Their works are tried by fire. This is the time of rewards and crowns. Revelation 19:9 says, "Blessed are those who are called to the marriage supper of the Lamb!" The saints will participate in this marriage feast. Not all will receive the crown. Some lazy and careless Christians will be ashamed to stand before the Lord without any reward. (1 John 2:28). The seven years of rejoicing in Heaven for the saints will be seven years of suffering and torture for the people in the world. THE GREAT TRIBULATION. THINK ABOUT THIS!!!

The signs of the coming of the Lord:
During the discussion Jesus had with His disciples on the Mount of Olives, in Matthew 24, He mentioned in verses 5 and 6, some occurrences which point to the beginning of wars and rumors of wars, famine and earthquakes. The Global Pandemic, COVID-19 may yet be another sign of the evils of the end-time. Looking for signs is no longer necessary; even the blind can discern this. Our greatest concern should be, to look inwards, to know if we are ready for the rapture. We do not know when it will happen. There is need for constant self- examination for without holiness no man shall see the Lord. The scripture admonishes us to watch and pray.

Qualification for the Rapture:
You must be Born Again. Live a transparent holy life. Live with eternity in view. Set your mind on the things above. Make peace with all men. Help the needy. Work for, and give to the work of God. Obey and do the word of God. Watch and pray for we know not when the Lord will come at death or the Rapture. (Micah 6:8; Matt. 24:42-44, 18:23-35; John 3:3; 4:35-38; 9:4; Heb.12:14).

The Great Tribulation:
Matt. 24:21-22, 29; Mark 13:19; Daniel 9:27; Revelation chapters 6-18. The great tribulation on earth begins as soon as the church is raptured. It will last for seven years. The first three and half years may be kind of peaceful. The anti-Christ will pretend to make peace. The unbelievers may think that the rapture was a good riddance of those who preached to them about salvation. There will be some Christians even church leaders who will not be raptured. This is why it is important to learn about this period of intense suffering and affliction which is reserved for the tribulation period. The Bible teaches that no known suffering can be compared to this. It is known as, "Jacob's trouble." The torture, severe pain and affliction will be so much that men will desire to die. "And in those days shall men seek death, and shall not find it; and shall desire to die, and death shall flee from them." (Revelation 6:9). Others will pray that the mountain will fall on them.
When Jesus came to the world, the Jews, His people rejected Him. They did not believe that He was the promised Messiah. The purpose of the great tribulation is to make Israel suffer so that they can cry out for help. They will cry out in repentance for a Savior. In their state of pain and sorrow, they will remember the promised Messiah. God in His mercy will forgive His children and Jesus will come and deliver them from their enemy, the devil.

Jesus is our Savior. The great tribulation is also to judge the unbelieving men and women of all ages. (Zechariah 12:10-11).

The wrath of God is on the world because they failed to believe in His Son Jesus Christ who paid the price for their sins. These unbelievers now have to pay the price for their sins. Unfortunately, the punishment has no end. It is for ever and ever. Here are a few scriptures that describe the wrath of God and the intensity of the affliction. Matt. 24: 21 "For then there will be great tribulation, such as has not been since the beginning of the world to this time, no, nor ever shall be."

Mark 13:19 "For in those days shall be affliction, such as was not from the beginning of the creation which God created unto this time, neither shall be."

Joel 2: 2a "A day of darkness and gloominess, a day of clouds and thick darkness, like the morning clouds spread over the mountains."

Zephaniah 1:15 "That day is a day of wrath, a day of trouble and distress, a day of devastation and desolation, a day of darkness and gloominess, a day of clouds and thick darkness."

Zephaniah 1:18 "Neither their silver nor their gold shall be able to deliver them in the day of the Lord's wrath; but the whole land shall be devoured by the fire of His jealousy: for He will make a speedy riddance of all those who dwell in the land."

Daniel's Prophesy of seventy weeks:
Daniel 9:24-27.
Daniel prophesied in the ninth chapter of his book that there will be seventy weeks from the rebuilding of Jerusalem to the end of time. This revelation was for Israel, God's chosen people. The Hebrew word 'week' means "a week of years," or seven years. Seventy weeks or seventy sevens is a period of 490 years. Some of the prophecies have been fulfilled; the rebuilding of Jerusalem as decreed by Cyrus; the atonement for sin, this was accomplished by the death of Jesus. Daniel 9:26 says, "the Messiah was cut off." This is also confirmed in Isaiah 53:8. After the death of Christ, the prince (the Antichrist) would make an agreement with the Jews for one week (seven years) to protect them from their enemies. This agreement will be reached in the 70th week which is yet to be fulfilled. The events of the prophesies up to the 69th week is fulfilled and many believe that the church age between the 69th and the 70th week was not revealed to Daniel. From this teaching we know that the tribulation period is seven years. The last week of Daniel's 'seventy weeks prophecy.'
2 Thess. 2:6-10 indicates that the antichrist cannot be revealed until the restrainer is taken out of the midst. The restrainer is the Holy Spirit in the church. Once the church is taken away, (the rapture) then Satan will place the antichrist in charge of the world system. The antichrist will make an agreement to protect the Jews for seven years but after three and half years (the middle of the seven years) he, Satan will break the agreement.

The abomination of desolation:
As the antichrist breaks his covenant with Israel, he becomes the world ruler, declares himself to be God and desecrates the temple in Jerusalem. (2 Thess. 2:3-4; Revelation 13:14-15). He will put a statue of himself in the temple and the false prophets will cause the whole

earth to worship it. He will severely persecute those who are loyal to Christ. Satan has always wanted the world's worship. (Matt. 4: 8-11). The antichrist will be worshiped by many in the middle of the tribulation. In Matt. 24:15, Jesus quoted from Daniel 9:27. The abomination of desolation refers to an unclean and sinful person (the antichrist), defiling the Holy Temple of God by physically seating in the temple and being worshiped as God. If the sacrifice of the wicked is an abomination to God, (Proverbs 15:8a) how much more the proclamation of a sinner as God in the place where God has put His name; the temple in Jerusalem. This desecration of the temple is the event that alerts the tribulation saints that the coming of the Son of God is imminent. (Let the reader understand).

The three and half years; the time and times and half the time; forty and two months:

These times are used to describe the period of affliction and intense suffering of the world. There will be dreadful persecution for those who remain loyal to Christ. (Revelation 11:6-7; 13:7,15-18) You will have to receive the "666" mark in order to buy or sell. There will be believers who missed the rapture, those that got converted during the tribulation and those who are against God.

The antichrist will have so much power (given to him by Satan) to perform miracles, signs and wonders. Many who do not know the truth and those who have no deep commitment to the truth of God's word will be deceived. (2 Thess. 2:9-12).

During the reign of the antichrist he will speak blasphemy. (Revelation 13:5-6). Do not be carried away by miracles, signs and wonders because some are from the enemy of our soul. Test the Spirit. I encourage every child of God to strive to draw closer to God. He will solve your problems and give you the grace and peace to continue to the end.

The battle of Armageddon (The Valley of Megiddo)
Daniel 11:45; Revelation 16:16.
The Antichrist was given power to perform many miracles, signs and wonders. He will become very proud and many nations will support him because of his false power and lying wonders. He will see himself as equal to God. In his pride, he will blaspheme. (Rev. 13:5-6). God will however not forsake His children. In Revelation 11:1-12, two witnesses were sent to preach the word and some received the message. Praise God!! Though the witnesses were killed, they completed their assignment. Their enemies watched them ascend to heaven.

At the end of the tribulation, Israel will repent having learnt their lesson in a very hard way. They will mourn and repent for their sins. They will cry for the Messiah to come and save them. God will hear their prayer and come as their Savior.

Satan will gather many nations at Armageddon under the direction of the antichrist, and make war against God and His people. This war will involve the entire world.

When that time comes, Christ will return and supernaturally intervene to destroy the antichrist, his armies and all who disobey God. (Revelation 19:15-21) Satan will be bound for one thousand years and Christ will establish His Kingdom on earth. Having become aware of the joy of a raptured saint and the suffering of the tribulation period, what manner of Christian should you be? (Read Revelations chapters 6 -18 over and over again). Jesus said it all, "Watch and pray." No one knows when the rapture or physical death will be. The tribulation saints will know when the Son of Man will come. Jesus said that they will know when they see the abomination of desolation standing in the holy place, (when the antichrist defiles the temple of God).

At the rapture, the trumpet will sound and the saints will meet the Lord in the air. (1 Thess. 4:16-18). At the second coming, the angels will gather the saints from the four corners of the earth at the sound of the trumpet. (Matt. 24:31). Both gathering will be preceded by the trumpet sound. Will you hear the trumpet sound? Do not be carried away by the pleasures of sin. Live your life with eternity in view. I pray that we will all be raptured. The great tribulation will not be our portion in Jesus name. Amen and Amen.

CHAPTER 15

THE MILLENNIUM, RESURRECTIONS AND JUDGMENTS

The great tribulation will end when Satan and his followers are defeated at the battle of Armageddon. (Revelation 19:15-21) All that our Lord has to do is speak the word, and "the sword of His mouth" will devour His enemies. Satan will be bound for 1000 years. "Then I saw an angel coming down from heaven, having the key to the bottomless pit and a great chain in his hand. He laid hold on the dragon, that serpent of old, who is the Devil and Satan, and bound him for a thousand years; and he cast him into the bottomless pit, and shut him up, and set a seal on him, so that he should deceive the nations no more till the thousand years were finished. But after these things he must be released for a little while." (Revelation 20:1-3 NKJV).

Christ reigns with His Saints: Revelation 20:4 – 6.
Having taken care of His enemies, Christ will establish His righteous kingdom on earth. The 1,000- year kingdom reign of Christ and His church is known as the millennium. At last, Christ and His church will reign over nations of the earth, and Israel will enjoy the blessings promised by the prophets.
(Isaiah 2:1-5, 4:1-6, 11:1-9, 12:1-6, 30:18-20, 35:1-10).

The purpose of the millennial kingdom: It will be the fulfillment of God's promise to Israel and to Jesus Christ. (Psalm 2; Luke1:30 -33). It will be a time of God's glory when all nature will be set free from the bondage of sin. (Romans 8:19-22). The original curse placed on mankind in Genesis will be removed. It will be an answer to our prayer, "thy Kingdom come on earth as it is in Heaven."

It will be a time to receive the blessings of participating in the first resurrection. "Blessed and holy is he who has part in the first resurrection. Over such the second death has no power, but they shall be priests of God and of Christ, and shall reign with Him a thousand years." (Revelation 20:6).
All our desires will be met during the millennium reign for there will be peace, unity, joy, long life, no wars, no famine and no oppression.

The inhabitants of the millennium:
Those who will live during the millennium reign are the glorified saints, the citizens of the nations who bow in submission to Christ. (Matt. 8:11; 25:31-40). The people will live long lives because the earth will be in perfect condition. (Isaiah 65: 18-25). They will marry and have children who are expected to conform to our Lord's righteous rule. As the millennium progresses, some will only pay lip service to the Lord. They will become easy prey for Satan when he is released after the 1,000 years. "Now when the thousand years is expired, Satan will be released from prison and will go out to deceive the nations which are in the four corners of the earth,
Gog and Magog to gather them together to battle, whose number is as the sand of the sea." (Revelation 20:8 NKJV).

Finally, brethren, let us work, let us toil and labor till the Master comes. It will be a shame if we do not reign with Christ. This is the time to prepare. Heaven is a prepared place for prepared people. Let us remind ourselves of the Lord's return. The saints of old reminded themselves of the Lord's return in their daily greetings which was (Maranatha) which means, O Lord, come!
(1 Corinthians 16:22c).

Resurrection of the dead:
Daniel. 12:2; Isaiah 26:19; John 5:28-29; 1 Corinthians 15:20; 1 Thess. 4: 13-16; Revelation 20:4,6,12-13.
All Christians believe that all who have ever lived and died will be resurrected, some to honor and glory and some to shame and contempt. Jesus said in John 5: 25, "Most assuredly, I say to you, the hour is coming, and now is, when the dead will hear the voice of the Son of God; and those who hear will live." (NKJV)
Jesus was the first to resurrect from the dead. He became the first fruit of all who died. (1 Corinthians 15:20).
The next group will be the resurrection of the church at the rapture. (1 Thess. 4:1-16). This is called the first resurrection. They held on to the end. Praise God!!!

The tribulation saints will resurrect at the end of the tribulation just before the millennial reign of Christ. (Matt. 24:31).
The resurrection of the unsaved is called the second resurrection. This resurrection takes place after the 1,000 years of Christ's reign. All unsaved dead from Adam to the end of the millennium will be included in this resurrection. (Revelation 20:11-15). They will be thrown into the lake of fire for ever and ever. Death and Hades will be thrown into the lake of fire.

The judgments:
"The Lord is our Judge; the Lord is our Lawgiver; the Lord is our King; He will save us." (Isaiah 33:22). As creator of the earth and its inhabitants, God alone has the prerogative to pass judgment on both. God judged the world in the days of Noah.

He judged the pride of those who were building the tower of Babel. He judged and destroyed Sodom and Gomorrah with its neigboring towns. The Bible warns individuals that they have only one chance to be reconciled to God before they face judgment. "And as it is appointed for man to die once, but after this the judgment." (Heb. 9:27). There are three judgments before the end of time.

1. The judgment seat of Christ: This occurs following the Rapture of the church. (1 Corinthians 3:12-15). The raptured saints are judged according to their works and they receive their crowns. They will participate in the marriage supper of the Lamb. (Revelation 19:9). This is a seven-year period. While the saints are rejoicing, the people on earth are undergoing untold hardship of the great tribulation.
2. The judgment of nations: The judgment of nations takes place at the end of the tribulation, just before the millennial Kingdom, when Christ has destroyed the armies of the world that had atempted to destroy Israel. (Revelation 19:11-21).
3. The Great White Throne Judgment: This is the final judgment. Satan will be released after the 1,000 years. He will continue his job of deceiving people and turning them against Christ. He will gather many nations for another battle, Gog and Magog to fight against Christ. Fire will come down from Heaven and devour them. Satan, the Devil, will be cast into the Lake of fire. (Revelations 20:7-10). "The Great White Throne Judgment will not resemble the courtroom of this world. There will be a Judge but no jury, a prosecution but no defense, a sentence but no appeal." (Warren W. Wiersbe). This is the judgment at which sinners stand in the presence of a holy and just God to give account of their sins. (Revelation 20:11-15). We view God as the God of love but He must deal with sin and sinners too.

Conclusion:

If we are wise, we will obey God and do His will. "He who has an ear, let him hear what the Spirit says to the churches." (Revelation 2:7). So, brothers and sisters do not envy the unbelievers who seem to have everything going well for them. Pray that they will be saved because they do not know that unless they repent, their end will be in the lake of fire.

CHAPTER 16

BACKSLIDING, A SERIOUS HINDRANCE

Backsliding is a stumbling block in our race to heaven. It is important that we pay careful attention to this topic. Backsliding is usually very gradual; this is why we should continually examine ourselves to know if we are still in the faith. Jesus praised the church in Ephesus, in Revelation 2:1 -7, for their good works but had one thing against them; "that you have lost your first love. Remember therefore from where you have fallen; repent and do the first works, or else I will come to you quickly and remove your lampstand from its place—unless you repent." God is not happy when His children backslide. Repentance is the way out or we will be treated as unbelievers. "No one, having put his hand to the plow, and looking back, is fit for the Kingdom of God." (Luke 9:62 NKJV).

What is backsliding?
1 Kings 11:9; Proverbs 14:14; Jeremiah 3:14,14:7; Matt. 24:12; Galatians 2:18.
Backsliding is falling from the spiritual height you had attained. It is a regression from being a vibrant Christian to being a lukewarm Christian. The church of the Laodiceans in Revelation 3, was referred to as a "lukewarm church" because they were neither hot nor cold. Christians are the salt of the world but if the salt loses its taste, it is useless. They are the light of the world, but if the day light becomes dim, how can others see the way? Galatians 2:18 says, "For if I build again those things which I destroyed; I make myself a transgressor." (NKJV). We all know that no transgressor has a place in the Kingdom of God.

No one is above backsliding. "Therefore, let him who thinks he stands take heed lest he fall." (1 Corinthians 10:12 NKJV). There are pastors, preachers, leaders, church workers who have backslidden but are still very active in the work of God. They may attend every meeting. Backsliding is from the heart. King Solomon was warned in 1Kings 11:2 not to intermarry with other nations around him because they will turn his heart after their gods. He ignored the warning and ended up a backslider. He turned his back to the God of his fathers and worshiped the many idols of his wives and concubines. King Solomon was commended in 1 Kings 3:3. "And Solomon loved the Lord, walking in the statutes of his father David." (NKJV). He obeyed God but at the end, he disobeyed God. How we end our spiritual race matters a lot. My prayer is that we will make it across the finish line. It is easy to condemn Solomon but we must remember that we backslide in prayer, in studying the word, in reaching out to the unsaved, in memorizing scriptures and in many other arears of our Christian walk. "Brethren, if a man is overtaken in any trespass, you who are spiritual restore such a one in a spirit of gentleness, considering yourself lest you also be tempted." (Galatians 6:1 NKJV).

Signs of backsliding:
1. **Spiritual pride:** When we believe that what we do is by our wisdom and strength. We fail to give God the glory. King Nebuchadnezzar was humiliated when he boasted about his greatness. (Proverbs 16:18; Daniel 4:28-30; James 4:6).
2. **No hunger for the word of God:** "Man shall not live by bread alone, but by every word that proceeds from the mouth of God." (Matt. 4:4 NKJV). You are backsliding if you are comfortable about not reading or studying the word of God for a day or more. (Job 23:12).

3. **The fire of prayer is going out:** The Bible instructs us to pray without ceasing. (1 Thess. 5:17). Luke 18:1 says, "Men ought always to pray and not to faint." When our private prayer is not as much as it used to be. You become lethargic and sometimes fall asleep during prayer meetings. When you lose interest in praying or prayer becomes difficult. Prayer should come from the heart.

4. **Love of pleasure:** When you begin to love the pleasure of the world. You begin to enjoy the things you once abstained from as a believer. (Galatians 2:18). "But she who lives in pleasure is dead while she lives" (1 Timothy 5:6) Love of pleasure will result in spiritual death.

5. **Loss of sense of guilt:** When you make excuses for your sins and may even quote some scriptures to support your evil behavior. You no longer see sin as sin. Justifying your sin instead of repenting is a sure sign of backsliding. (1 Timothy 4:1-2).

6. **Approving the sins of others:** When you cannot tell other believers their sins according to the word of God. You should love the sinner but hate his sins. The sin of compromise is a sign of backsliding. The church in Pergamos in Revelation 2:14-16, was warned about compromising. The Lord will fight against them with the sword of His mouth if they don't repent.

7. **Bearing the fruit of the flesh:** You are backsliding when you fulfil the desires of the flesh. "I say then: Walk in the Spirit, and you shall not fulfil the lust of the flesh. For the flesh lusts against the Spirit, and the Spirit against the flesh, and these are contrary to one another, so that you do not do the things that you wish." (Galatians 5:16 -17. NKJV).

8. **Giving the world a first place in your life:** (1John 2:15 -17; Luke16:13; Matt.16:26). When a believer's waking thought is about making more money, acquiring more worldly goods and following the fashions of the world, he is backsliding. "For the love of money is a root of all

kinds of evil, for which some have strayed from the faith in their greediness, and pierced themselves through with many sorrows." (1 Timothy 6:10 NKJV). "He who loves silver will not be satisfied with silver; nor he who loves abundance, with increase. This also is vanity." (Eccl. 5:10 NKJV). "You are those who justify yourselves before men, but God knows your hearts. For what is highly esteemed among men is an abomination in the sight of God." (Luke. 16:15). All good gifts come from above. God has promised to take care of us. He takes care of the birds of the air and makes the flowers beautiful. (Matt. 6:31-34)

9. **Living the life that please men:** No hypocrite has a place in the Kingdom of God. A hypocrite preaches one thing and does another. He honors God with his lips but his heart is far away from God. He is a backslider.

10. **No passion for lost souls:** A believer is commissioned to tell others about Jesus, our only Savior. When a believer is not concerned about the souls that will perish in hell, he is backsliding. (Mark 16:15-18; Matt. 28:19-20; Ezekiel 33: 6-9).

How to return to God:
Isaiah 55:6 – 7; 1:18-20; Hosea 10:12; Luke 15:11-24.
If a backslider does not return to God, he may continue to the state of apostacy. This is dangerous. As soon as we notice any of the signs of backslidding in our Christian walk, we should arise like the prodigal son in Luke 15 and seek the face of God. "I will arise and go unto my father" and he arose and came to his father. Search your heart to know what you did wrong or what you indulged in which affected your spiritual walk. "Remember therefore from where you have fallen; repent and do the first work." (Revelation 2:5 NKJV). You may have backslidden in more than one aspect. Think of the things you did before which helped your spiritual growth. You may have to take the same route to get back to the Lord. The sin of backsliding is like

a chain. It pulls other sins along. Be encouraged as you struggle to return to the Lord because God has promised to heal our backslidings. Jeremiah 3:22 says, "Return, you backsliding children, and I will heal your backslidings." Hosea 14:4 says, "I will heal their backsliding; I will love them freely, for my anger is turned away from him." There is hope. God needs your heart. Proverbs 23:26 says, "My son, give me your heart, and let your eyes observe my ways." (NKJV).

Make a timetable for your prayer: Endeavour to keep to the time you allotted to prayer. Start with 15 to 20 mins then increase gradually to 30 mins or 1 hour. Read a few verses of scripture over and over again. Meditate on the verses of scripture you have read. You may need to write it down. Have a time to read or listen to 2 to 4 chapters of the Bible every day.

Have a prayer partner: This is a way to have someone to lift you up at the time you may be feeling faint. You may also want to have a partner with whom you can share scriptures you have memorized. Do all you can to be restored. Sometimes have a night vigil. Prayer and fasting will help. These are ways you can seek the face of God.
It may have taken months or years before you noticed that you are not where you are supposed to be spiritually. Lots of church activities may have led you to backslide. Do not expect to be restored in one day or even in one month. God knows about you and will answer your prayers in due season. Do not give up. Do not faint. (Isaiah 40:28 – 31). We do not know when the Lord will come for His own. It will be of great help if you call a friend, a brother or sister to share what you read during your morning devotion. When your confidence in praying and understanding the word of God is restored, you can call an unsaved neighbor or family member and tell them about the need to become born again.

Sing praises to God always. The Holy Spirit may take over and you wake up to the Spirit of God singing in your heart. Alleluia. Attend a good fellowship where the word of God is not adulterated. Always ask questions to have a better understanding of the teaching. Search the scriptures for the truth. (John 5:39; Acts 17:11). As you desire to draw nearer to the Lord, the Holy Spirit will be there for you if you ask Him. (Luke 11:13).

Finally, remember that the enemy will not want you to return to God. Equip yourself with the whole armor of God. Do not give Satan a chance. He led you to the backslidden state you are struggling to defeat. The good news is that Jesus has defeated Satan. "For this purpose, the Son of man was manifested, that He might destroy the works of the devil." (1 John 3:8b).
If you are still having a sweet fellowship with the Lord, I rejoice with you. Keep it up. Here are choruses to two hymns I love to sing. They help me to keep holding on. (1) "Trust and obey, for there's no other way to be happy in Jesus, but to trust and obey. ." (2) "Never give up, never give up, never give up to thy sorrows, Jesus will bid them depart; Trust in the Lord, trust in the Lord. Sing when your trials are greatest. Trust in the Lord and take heart." May the Holy Spirit continue to lead, teach, guide and guard us in this walk with our God. His grace is always sufficient for us in Jesus name. Amen.

CHAPTER 17

INTERCESSORS NEEDED

Two Kingdoms at war:
We hear about wars in the news but the reality of the war only strikes when we or someone we know becomes a casualty. The moment you make a 'U-turn' in your life and turn to Jesus, you are also turning into a battlefield. We were all in darkness under the rule of Satan before we came to know Jesus. This turn from Satan to Jesus makes Satan very angry with every believer in Christ. He puts stumbling blocks on our way to make us fall and come back to him. All believers are engaged in a very real spiritual battle between the Kingdom of God and the kingdom of Satan. We know who God is. He is the creator of all things. He is the King of kings. He is Omnipotent, Omnipresent and Omniscient. There are many names for our God, which cannot all be contained in this book.

But who is Satan? Satan has many names none of which is good. He is a disobedient creature of God. He was a very powerful angel in Heaven but when he rebelled against God, God sent him down to the world pending when he will be thrown into the lake of fire. As with all rebellions, about one third of the angels took sides with Satan. They too were sent down to the world with their leader. This is why he is called the "god of this world." (2 Corinthians 4:3-4). Satan means adversary, because he is the enemy of God and His children. He is the Devil. Devil means accuser. He accuses the brethren day and night. (Revelation 12:10). He is the tempter. (Matt. 4:3) He is called the murderer and the liar. (John 8:44). He is compared to a serpent; a lion and he transforms himself into "an angel of light."

(Genesis 3:1; Revelation 12:9; 1 Peter 5:8; 2 Corinthians 11:13-15). Since Satan is a created being, he is limited in knowledge and what he does.

Satan has a well-organized network of helpers. He and his cohorts are continually attacking believers. This is a spiritual warfare. Apostle Paul explains this in Ephesians 6:12. "For we do not wrestle against flesh and blood, but against principalities, against powers, against the rulers of the darkness of this age, against spiritual hosts of wickedness in the heavenly places." (NKJV). In 2 Corinthians 10:3-4, Paul writes "For though we walk in the flesh, we do not war according to the flesh. For the weapons of our warfare are not carnal but mighty in God for pulling down strongholds." (NKJV). We know that Satan is strong and powerful but his power cannot be compared to the strength and power of God. Since our warfare is mighty in God, we are sure of victory even before the battle starts. Jesus, Our Commander in Chief, has defeated Satan and his cohorts. "Having disarmed principalities and powers, He made a public spectacle of them, triumphing over them in it." (Colossians 2:15).

Satan attacks believers from three different fronts. 1 John 2:15-17 says, "Do not love the world or the things in the world. If anyone loves the world, the love of the Father is not in him. For all that is in the world- the lust of the flesh, the lust of the eyes, and the pride of life – is not of the Father but is of the world. And the world is passing away, and the lust of it, but he who does the will of God abides forever." (NKJV). This is the device of Satan. In the book of Genesis, Satan tempted Eve using these three methods, "So when the woman saw that the tree was good for food, (the lust of the flesh) that it was pleasant to the eyes, (the lust of the eyes) and a tree desirable to make one wise, (the pride of life) she took of the fruit and ate." (Genesis 3:6 NKJV). In the temptation of Jesus, Satan used the same device.

He wanted Jesus to turn the stone into bread and eat because he knew that Jesus was hungry. He also promised to give Jesus all the kingdoms he does not own, if Jesus would fall down from the mountain and worship him. (Matt. 4:1-10). To tempt King David, he used the lust of the eye. "He saw a woman washing herself." The eye is the gateway to the mind. The Devil will love to use our eyes to lure us to sin.

The sin of "the pride of life" is the arrogant desire to be recognized. It is seen in the desires we exhibit, trying to outdo others in spending and getting, wanting the first place at every gathering; seeking positions and taking titles and names that belittle the people around you. You cannot compete with the world and still be a child of God. "Pride goes before destruction, and a haughty spirit before a fall." (Proverbs16:18)

Brethren since we know that Satan always wants to use the good desires God has given us to make us commit sin, we must be vigilant. We become partakers of the divine nature when we accept Jesus as our Lord and Savior. Therefore, a believer has the old nature (flesh) and the new nature (Spirit). We are to walk in the Spirit because our Father is a Spirit. The flesh (human nature) tries to prevent us from yielding to the Spirit. "I say then; walk in the Spirit, and you shall not fulfill the lust of the flesh. For the flesh lusts against the Spirit, and the Spirit against the flesh; and these are contrary one to another; so that you do not do the things that you wish. But if you are led by the Spirit, you are not under the law" (Galatians 5:16-18 NKJV).

The great need for intercessors:
Isaiah 59:16; Ezekiel 22:30; Romans 8:26-27; 2 Corinthians 10:1- 6; Ephesians 6:12-18; Hebrews 7:25.

Jesus can use even His breath to defeat Satan but He wants His children to participate in this battle. Paul used the armor of the Roman soldier to describe how a Christian should be dressed for the spiritual battle.
Ephesians 6:13 - 17 lists the armor to put on.
(1). "The belt of truth: Jesus is the Truth. Satan is a liar. A believer who lives by the truth can face the enemy without fear.
(2). The breastplate of righteousness: The breastplate protects the heart of the soldier. Our righteousness is in Christ (Ephesians 4:24; 2 Corinthians 5:21; Philippians 3:9). Righteousness protects our spiritual life.
(3). Feet protected by the gospel of peace: The peace of God gives us security. We can win the battle as we share the gospel of peace with the lost world. (Philippians 4:7; Romans 10:15).
(4). The shield of faith: Faith is a defensive weapon that protects us from the fiery darts of our enemy.
The faith mentioned here is a 'living faith.' This is the faith which makes us trust in the promises and power of God. It enables us live by faith.
(5). The helmet of Salvation: The helmet refers to the mind controlled by God. We are to "grow in grace, and in the knowledge of our Lord and Savior Jesus Christ." (2 Peter 3:18). The primary battlefield is the Christian mind. If we equip ourselves with the truth of God's word, Satan cannot lure us into sin through doubt and unbelief." (The Jeremiah Study Bible).
(6). The sword of the Spirit: This is the word of God. It is the only offensive weapon. Jesus used it to defeat Satan when He was

tempted in Matt. 4: 1-10. Paul teachés us in Hebrews 4:12 that God's word is sharper than a two-edged sword. "For the word of God is living and powerful, and sharper than any two-edged sword, piercing even to the division of soul and spirit, and of joints and marrow, and is a discerner of the thoughts and the intents of the heart."
We receive and put on the whole armor of God at salvation. This is the same as putting on our Lord Jesus Christ. The whole armor is the picture of Jesus Christ. Jesus is the Truth. (John 14:6). He is our righteousness. (2 Corinthians 5:21). He is our peace. (Ephesians 2:14). He is our faith. Paul says in Galatians 2:20c, "and the life which I now live in the flesh I live by faith in the Son of God, who loved me and gave Himself for me." Jesus is the Captain of our salvation. (Hebrews 2:10). He is the word of God. (John 1:1,14; Revelation 19:13). Since Jesus is our armor, we should put Him on every day by renewing our strength in Him.

Knowing that God has equipped us for the battle which He has already won, believers are encouraged to make themselves available for this spiritual warfare. In the days of Ezekiel and Isaiah God was looking for a man to stand in the gap and intercede for nations. (Ezekiel 22:30; Isaiah 59:16). The Bible says, that God found no intercessor. God is still looking for believers who will set themselves apart for this ministry of intercession. "Epaphras, who is one of you, a bond-servant of Christ, greets you, always laboring fervently for you in prayers, that you may stand perfect and complete in all the will of God. For I bear him witness that he has a great zeal for you, and those who are in Laodicea, and those in Hierapolis." (Colo. 4:12 NKJV). God wants us to pray for the unsaved and for believers. Jesus gave a prayer request in Matt. 9: 37-38, "The harvest truly is plentiful, but the laborers are few. Therefore, pray the Lord of the harvest to send out laborers into the harvest."

Paul in 1 Timothy 2:2, wants us to pray for all in authority. In Ephesians 6:18 he says, we should pray for saints and the ministers of the word. If we allow God to use us as intercessors, we will be laying treasures in heaven where thieves will not have access.

The characteristics of a prayer warrior or an intercessor:

(1). He must be born again and living in newness of life. The old man is buried and he is no longer attracted by the things of this world. "The effective fervent prayer of a righteous man avails much." (James 5:16b)
(2). He is set apart for the service of the Kingdom. He is a faithful worker.
(3). He has the mind of Christ. He loves the sinner but hates his sins. Has a zealous love for people. (The more we love people the more we pray for them). He sees the perishing world and is ready to sacrifice whatever it takes to rescue the people. He has passion for the lost.
(4). He studies the word and uses it as the weapon to challenge the enemy. (2 Timothy 2:15).
(5). He waits on the Lord for renewed grace, strength and power. He prays for fresh anointing daily.
(6). Even though God wants those who will stand in the gap, He encourages us to pray for the baptism in the Holy Spirit. We need the power of the Holy Spirit. "But you shall receive power when the Holy Spirit has come upon you;" (Acts 1:8a) Just as the disciples of old tarried in Jerusalem until they were endured with power from on high so we should wait on the Lord. (Luke 24:49).

Our God has promised to give us the Holy Spirit if only we ask Him. Luke 11:13 says, "If you then, being evil, know how to give good gifts to your children, how much more will your heavenly Father give the Holy Spirit to those who ask Him?"

My brothers and sisters, God has provided us with all we need to become effective intercessors or prayer warriors. Jesus has won the battle already. He has given us the weapon for this spiritual battle. He has given us the Holy Spirit to teach, guide, and pray through us. (John 14: 26; Romans 8: 26). Jesus is continually interceding on our behalf. (John 16:23; Romans 8:34, Hebrews 7:25). Don't you think it will be good to pray along with Jesus? Think of the eternal reward!

CHAPTER 18

HOME AT LAST: HEAVEN OR HELL

God has revealed to us in the Bible all about our eternal home. Many are scared to read the book of Revelation. It contains the prophecies that will give us more understanding of God's purpose for the redeemed and the unbelievers. Revelation 21:1-2 says, "Now I saw a new heaven and a new earth, for the first heaven and the first earth had passed away. Also, there was no more sea. Then I, John, saw the holy city, New Jerusalem, coming down out of heaven from God, prepared as a bride adorned for her husband. And I heard a loud voice from heaven saying, "Behold, the tabernacle of God is with men, and He will dwell with them, and they shall be His people. God Himself will be with them and be their God." From the scripture quoted above we know that God wants to live on earth with His children, the redeemed. All genuine believers groan for a better place. Father Abraham waited for a city which has foundations whose builder and maker is God. (Hebrews 11:10; Philippians 3:20).

God cannot live in a defiled and polluted earth, for He is Holy. Isaiah 65:17–19 says, "For behold, I create new heavens and a new earth; And the former shall not be remembered or come to mind. But be glad and rejoice forever in what I create; For behold, I create Jerusalem as a rejoicing, and her people a joy. I will rejoice in Jerusalem, and joy in My people, the voice of weeping shall no longer be heard in her nor the voice of crying." This means that the present earth will be destroyed because it is polluted by our sins and wickedness. The stars and galaxies, heaven and earth will be shaken (Haggai 2:6; Hebrews 12: 26-28), and will vanish like smoke. (Isaiah 51:6).

2 Peter 3:7 reads "But the heavens and the earth which are now preserved by the same word, are reserved for fire until the day of judgement and perdition of ungodly men." (Read 2 Peter 3:10- 14). My brothers and sisters take a good look at all the magnificent buildings, malls, entertainment centers, all will melt in fervent heat on the day of the Lord. All the wonders of the world will be consumed by fire. (Isaiah 51:6, 66:22; Psalm 102:25-26; Romans 8:19-22; Hebrews 1:10-12, 12:27).

At the first resurrection, the graves of the believers are empty. The tribulation saints resurrect at the end of the tribulation just before the millennium. The graves of all the unbelievers are also empty as they resurrect to stand before the Great White Throne Judgment. In preparation for the coming down of the New Jerusalem everywhere must be clean and pure, even under the earth, where humans were buried. It will be wise for us to lay our treasures in heaven. "Do not lay up for yourselves treasures on earth, where moth and rust destroy and where thieves break in and steal; but lay up for yourselves treasures in heaven, where neither moth nor rust destroys and where thieves do not break in and steal. For where your treasure is there your heart will be also." (Matt. 6:19-21).

Jesus said in Matt. 24:35, "Heaven and earth will pass away; but My words will by no means pass away." What does this mean? It means that what He said in John 3:3, "Most assuredly, I say to you, unless one is born again, he cannot see the Kingdom of God." This Word of God must be fulfilled. (John 1:12). "But as many as received Him, to them He gave power to become the sons of God." This word of God must come to pass. John 10:9, "I am the door. If anyone enters by Me, he will be saved, and will go in and out and find pasture." Again, "He who believes in the Son has everlasting life; and he who does not believe the Son shall not see life, but the wrath of God abides on him." (John 3:36). Knowing that Jesus Christ is the same yesterday, today and forever, and that His word is forever settled in Heaven, it will be wise to do what He says we should do. (Hebrews 13:8; Psalm 119:89). God will not lower His standard to please us. Remember that He is the unchangeable God. Some call Him the 'unchanging changer.' Yes, He can change our ugly situations and make them beautiful. (He will heal the sick, provide and protect you and answer your prayers). He will however not change His written or spoken word. Our God is no respecter of persons!

Who are those qualified to live with God in the New Jerusalem?
All sinners who have repented of their sins and believe in the Lord Jesus Christ will be qualified to live with God in the New Jerusalem. Those who obey His word and do His will. "If you continue in My word, then are you My disciples indeed." (John 8:31).
Believers who have endured to the end. Those who by the grace of God, have overcome the world. "He who overcomes shall inherit all things, and I will be His God and he shall be My son." (Revelation 21:7). If you are in Christ now, you must meditate on this scripture (1 Corinthians 10:12) "Therefore let him who thinks he stands take heed lest he fall."

A glimpse of Heaven: Revelation 21:1-26; 22:1-5.
I run a Bible Study/Prayer conference line Ministry in the United States of America. Most of my fellowship members are senior citizens. The oldest member is 96. I have some younger ones in their forties and fifties. One evening while I was teaching about the beauty of heaven and why we must endeavor to make heaven; a voice murmured, "Have you been there?" I quickly picked that up and explained that all I teach is in the Bible. I have not been to

heaven but the book of Revelation has everything I need to know about heaven.

Heaven is a large and tangible City. Where we refer to as heaven today is not the heaven Jesus has gone to prepare the mansions for believers. Apostle John saw the Holy City coming down. "Then I, John, saw the holy city, New Jerusalem, coming down out of Heaven from God, prepared as a bride adorned for her husband." (Revelation 21:2). At the end of everything the New Heaven comes down to the new earth and God Himself will dwell with His children forever. (Revelation 21:3).

There will be no sin in Heaven: Satan, the tempter and all his followers would have been banished into the lake of fire after the final judgment at the Great White Throne Judgment. (Revelation 21:8).

The beautiful city and her features: Apostle John lacked words to describe the beauty he admired. I do too. He tells us about the many precious stones. The streets are of pure gold and transparent glass. The wall is high and has twelve gates. Each gate has the name of one of the twelve tribes of Israel etched into it. On the twelve foundations are the names of the twelve apostles. The foundations of the wall are adorned with all kinds of precious stones. This is what Judas missed and Mathias took his place. May no one take our place in Jesus name. The city is square. There is no house of worship, "for the Lord God Almighty and the Lamb are its temple," There is no need for the sun or the moon for "the Lamb is its light." (Revelation 21:22-23.) The city gates are never shut. There will be no night there. The redeemed shall walk in the light and the kings of the earth bring their glory and honor into it. In Revelation 22:1-5, the Bible tells us about a river of life from the throne of God, watering trees that bear twelve manner of fruits for the inhabitants. The leaves of the trees are for the healing of nations. The servants of God will have a fulfilling work to do. "And they shall reign for ever and ever."

How do you view Heaven?
If you call Heaven a city, you will think of its inhabitants; if you call it a Kingdom; you will think of its orderliness; if you call it Paradise, you will imagine its beauty. When you call it your Father's house, you will appreciate His love for you and seek His embrace and call Him, "Abba Father". The joy of Heaven, the New Jerusalem is that God and the Lamb will be with us forever.

Hell, the eternal home of Satan and all who reject Christ:
Psalm 9:17; Matt. 5:22,30; 25:46; Mark 9:43 -47; Luke 12:4 - 5; 16:20- 31; Revelation 14:10-11, 20:10, 12-15.

The scripture will not be complete without teaching about Hell. The purpose of teaching about Hell is to help everyone flee from sin so that we do not become candidates for or residents in hell. Hell is a place of everlasting punishment and torture. It is a place prepared for the devil and his angels. "Then He will also say to those on the left hand, 'Depart from Me, you cursed, into the everlasting fire prepared for the devil and his angels." (Matt. 25:41). God decreed that the wicked and those who reject Christ will be cast into hell fire." It will surprise you to hear that all the people in hell are believers in Christ. They believed after they died. It was too late. This is the time to believe on Him. The just shall live by faith. No sinner can condemn God for casting him into hell. God has provided a way of escape. Faith in Jesus is the only way to salvation.

When a sinner dies his soul immediately goes to hell. "And as it is appointed for men to die once, but after this the judgment." (Hebrews 9:27) This scripture confirms that the concept of purgatory is not biblical nor the notion of annihilation of the wicked. The sinner undergoes torture and excruciating pain in hell. His memory is alert.

(Luke 16:23-24). The pain is worse when you realize that you had the opportunity to turn to Christ but failed to do so. No one in hell will want his loved ones to experience the same pain. The rich man remembered his five brothers and wanted Lazarus to go to the earth and tell them to repent and flee from sin. "Then he said, I beg you therefore father, that you would send him (Lazarus) to my father's house, for I have five brothers, that he may testify to them, lest they also come to this place of torment. Abraham said to him, 'They have Moses and the prophets; let them hear them.' And he said, 'No, father Abraham, but if one goes to them from the dead, they will repent.' But he said to him, 'If they do not hear Moses and the prophets, neither will they be persuaded though one rise from the dead." (Luke 16:27-31).

Some doubt the existence of hell as a place of torture. They say that God is a merciful Father and so will not punish His children in hell. Someone said "If you believe, you receive. If you doubt, you do without." You that doubt the word of God, I plead with you to come to Jesus now for your double mindedness will lead you to where you will regret at last. Jesus talked and warned us about hell and the everlasting pain. The Apostles were not silent. (Matt. 7:15-19, 25:41, 46, 3:7-10; Romans 2:5, 9; 2 Thess. 1: 8-9; Hebrews 10: 26-27; James 3:5-6; 2 Peter 2:4-9, 3:7). Those who after reading the words of Jesus and the prophets, still doubt the existence of hell, are already on their way to experience the torture of hell unless they repent. Remember that the torture of hell is for ever and ever.

Who is the Judge at the Great White Judgment Throne?
Rev. 20:11-15.

The Judge is Jesus Christ, for the Father has committed all judgment to Him. (John 5:26-27; Acts 17:31). Jesus is the one that paid the price for the sins of the whole world. The lost sinners rejected Christ in life, now they must be judged by Him and face eternal damnation. Jesus will judge these unsaved people on the basis of what is written in the books. For sure one of the books will be the 'Bible.' "He who rejects Me, and does not receive My words, has that which judges him- the word that I have spoken will judge him on the last day." (John 12:48). The Bible is for everyone to read. "You search the scriptures, for in them you think you have eternal life, and these are they which testify of Me." (John 5:39). You cannot blame your leaders. Everyone will give account of his life.
I believe that there are degrees of punishment in hell. (Matt.11:20-24). Each lost sinner will receive just punishment for Jesus judges us in righteousness. None can argue with Him or question His decision.

Conclusion:
Hell is where the devil and his angels will spend eternity. If we do not repent of our sins and accept Jesus who paid the price for our sins as our Lord and Savior, we make ourselves enemies of God. Satan or the devil is an enemy of God. If you are an enemy of God, you are in the same camp as Satan. The eternal home of the lost is portrayed as a place of "tribulation and anguish" (Romans 2:9); "Weeping and gnashing of teeth." (Matt. 22:13, 25:30). "Everlasting destruction" (2 Thess. 1:9) "A furnace of fire" (Matt.13:42, 50). Peter describes it as "chains of darkness." (2 Peter 2:4). Revelation 19:20 refers to it as a "lake of fire burning with brimstone." "It is a fearful thing to fall into the hands of the Living God." (Hebrews 10:31).

Though our God is merciful, He is also a consuming fire. Accept that you are the lost sinner whom Jesus came to save.

Jesus came for the sinners and not for the righteous. "I have not come to call the righteous, but sinners to repentance." (Luke 5:32). "As many as I love, I rebuke and chasten. Therefore, be zealous and repent. Behold, I stand at the door and knock. If anyone hears My voice and opens the door, I will come in to him and dine with him, and he with Me." (Revelation 3:19-20). God's grace is available now. Do not delay. Jesus is waiting at the door of your heart. Open the door of your heart and let Him in.

The Psalmist says, that we are fearfully and wonderfully made. You are too beautiful to perish in hell "where their worm does not die and the fire is not quenched." (Mark 9:44). I pray the lyrics of the hymn on the next page by John A. Sammi will help you think of where you will spend eternity.

Just Obey
by John A. Sammi

(1) Just as God who reigns on high,
Spake to men in days gone by;
So, the Lord is calling men today;
And, my brother, this is true,
Whatso'er he says to you,
There is but one thing to do---
Just Obey.

Chorus: Just obey---------Just obey
Is the way ----, God's way
When His message comes to you,
There is but one thing to do,
Just Obey. Just obey.

(2) If you're in the Savior's hands,
You must do as He commands,
For there is no other gospel way;
Never put the message by,
Never stop to reason 'why.'
When the Savior speaks to you---
Just obey.

(3) If for mansions fair you sigh,
In that land beyond the sky,
After time with you has pass'd away;
Tho' the way you may not see,
Christ is calling, "Follow Me,"
Faith and duty both will cry—
Just Obey.

CHAPTER 19

WHAT A FRIEND WE HAVE IN JESUS

Jesus is a perfect friend whom everyone must have. He loves us but hates our sins. The moment we separate ourselves from sin, Jesus becomes our best friend. In Luke 12:31 Jesus admonishes us to seek first the Kingdom of God and all our other desires will be fulfilled. "Do not fear little flock, for it is your Father's good pleasure to give you the Kingdom" (Luke 12:32). Jesus confirms that God the Father loves us and will give us the Kingdom. All we need to do is to obey His Word. If the Father wants to give us the Kingdom, let us prepare for our journey back home now that we have the time to do so. Jesus made our journey easier. When He said, "Come to Me, all you who labor and are heavy laden and I will give you rest. Take My yoke upon you and learn from Me, for I am gentle and lowly in heart, and you will find rest for your souls. For My yoke is easy and My burden is light." (Matt. 11:28 -30). Jesus is our friend indeed. He does not want us to perish.

When Jesus was on earth He ate with sinners. (Mark 2:15-17; Luke 5: 31-32,11:37,14:1,19:7). The Pharisees were held in high esteem in the society in the days of Jesus but they would not have anything to do with those they regarded as sinners. Almost everyone looked up to them for an explanation of the law and tradition. They were very proud and arrogant. The people knew that Jesus was righteous by His behavior and what He preached. They were amazed and confused when Jesus did not comport Himself like the Pharisees. They expected that Jesus would exalt Himself higher than the leaders of their time. When Jesus associated with tax collectors and

Publicans, they (the Pharisees) regarded Jesus as an unrighteous man.

Jesus explained to His accusers that He came for sinners and not for the righteous, for the sick and not for the healthy. He came for the unrighteous and not for the righteous. (Mark 2:17; Luke 5:31-32; John 3:17). "Now it happened, as He was dining in Levi's house, that many tax collectors and sinners also sat together with Jesus and His disciples, for there were many, and they followed Him. And when the scribes and Pharisees saw Him eating with the tax collectors and sinners, they said to His disciples, "How is it that He eats and drinks with tax collectors and sinners?" When Jesus heard it, He said to them, "Those who are well have no need of a physician, but those who are sick. I did not come to call the righteous, but sinners to repentance." (Mark 2:15-17). Our joy is that Jesus came for everybody. All have sinned and missed the mark set by God. We have come short of His glory. It is not too late to turn to Jesus. His grace is still available. Now is the day of salvation. If you make Jesus your friend today, you can be sure that you are a 'heaven bound' passenger.

Why did Jesus eat with sinners?

Jesus chose to eat with sinners so He could have a one on one conversation with them and He could talk to them about repentance and forgiveness. Jesus came to the world to save those who recognize that they have sinned and need a savior. Jesus is the Savior. He went to those who needed Him.
When Levi and Zacchaeus followed Jesus, many tax collectors came to Jesus. Jesus performed many miracles. For every miracle He performed, many people sought to see Him. His disciples increased.

Jesus used every occasion to preach about repentance and forgiveness. He healed the leper, touching the untouchable. Acts 10:38 summarizes the work of Jesus, "how God anointed Jesus of Nazareth with the Holy Spirit and with power, who went about doing good and healing all who were oppressed by the devil, for God was with Him." Wow!!! Just imagine Jesus coming into your house today and rolling away all the stumbling blocks in your way. May He visit you today to heal the sick and provide for you and your family. Don't forget to ask Him to open your spiritual eyes to see and know how to make Heaven your eternal home.

Here are a few verses of scripture that will help you understand that Jesus wants you to be His friend. He cares for you. "Therefore, humble yourselves under the mighty hand of God, that He may exalt you in due time, casting all your care upon Him, for He cares for you." (1 Peter 5:6-7)

Psalm 138:8a, "The Lord will perfect that which concerns me."

1 Corinthians 10:13, "No temptation has overtaken you except such as is common to man; but God is faithful, who will not allow you to be tempted beyond what you are able, but with the temptation will also make the way of escape, that you may be able to bear it."

Isaiah 41:10, "Fear not for I am with you; Do not be dismayed; for I am your God, I will strengthen you, Yes, I will help you, I will uphold you with My righteous right hand."

Isaiah 43:2, "When you pass through the waters, I will be with you; And through the rivers, they shall not overflow you. When you walk through the fire, you shall not be burned, nor shall the flame scorch you."

John 14:1-3, "Let not your heart be troubled, you believe in God, believe also in Me. In my Father's house are many mansions; if it were not so, I would have told you. I go to prepare a place for you. And if I go and prepare a place for you, I will come again and receive you to Myself; that where I am, there you may be also." (NKJV).

My brothers and sisters, Jesus has promised to give us abundant life. If you will make Jesus your best friend today, you will enjoy life here on earth and even more in Heaven. There will be challenges but He will make a way of escape. Heaven is a beautiful place which no one should miss!! "If then you were raised with Christ, seek those things which are above, where Christ is, sitting at the right hand of God. Set your mind on things above, not on things on earth. For you died, and your life is hidden with Christ in God. When Christ who is our life appears, then you also will appear with Him in glory." (Colossians 3:1-4). "Beloved, now we are children of God; and it has not yet been revealed what we shall be, but we know that when He is revealed, we shall be like Him, for we shall see Him as He is. And everyone who has this hope in Him purifies himself, just as He is pure." (1 John 3:2-3). Brethren, be ready and wait for the Captain of our Salvation. He will take us home! Alleluia! Alleluia!! Alleluia!!!

A benediction from Jude verses 24 -25, "Now to Him who is able to keep you from stumbling, and to present you faultless before the presence of His glory with exceeding joy. To God our Savior, who alone is wise, be glory and majesty, Dominion and power, both now and forever. Amen".

The hymn "I must tell Jesus" by Elisha A. Hoffman reveals the close relationship we should have with Jesus.

I MUST TELL JESUS
By Elisha A. Hoffman

1   I must tell Jesus all of my trials;
        I cannot bear these burdens alone;
        In my distress He kindly will help me;
        He ever loves and cares for His own.

Chorus: I must tell Jesus! I must tell Jesus!
        I cannot bear my burdens alone:
        I must tell Jesus! I must tell Jesus!
        Jesus can help me, Jesus alone.

2   I must tell Jesus all of my troubles;
        He is a Kind, compassionate Friend;
        If I but ask Him, He will deliver,
        Make of my troubles quickly an end.

3   Tempted and tried, I need a great Savior,
        One who can help my burdens to bear;
        I must tell Jesus; I must tell Jesus;
        He all my cares and sorrows will share.

4   O how the world to evil allures me!
        O how my heart is tempted to sin!
        I must tell Jesus, and He will help me
        Over the world the vict'ry to win.

About the Author

Rose Nkeiruka Mbamali was born into an Anglican and Catholic Family from Onitsha, Anambra State, Nigeria in October 1940. She attended Catholic schools from Elementary through Teacher's Training College. In 1960, she was among a select group of Catholics who embarked on a pilgrimage to Fatima in Portugal, Lourdes in France and the Vatican City in Rome, where she had the opportunity to meet Pope John XXIII. She became a Teacher in 1963 and taught several subjects at Loretto Teacher's Training College in Adazi, Anambra State, Nigeria, including the Liturgy of the Catholic church.

She relocated to Lagos in 1964 and got married to Joseph E. Mbamali in April of the same year. While in Lagos she worked in various positions at the Catholic Secretariat before returning to teaching.

In 1987 she heard a messagge "The key that unlocks Heaven's door" by W.F Kumuyi, the General Superintendent of the Deeper Christian Life Ministry. This message led her to give her life to Christ in November 8th, 1987. She became a member of the Deeper Christian Life Ministry in 1987, and was a leader in the Ministry for about 15 years before emigrating to the United States in 2003.
She remained committed to her deep faith in Christ, and in 2008 went on a pilgrimage to Israel. The prilgrimage strengthened her faith even more.

She lost her first son, Ikechukwu Mbamali on February 21st, 2011. Her deep faith in Christ and conviction that her son prepared well for the journey to Heaven gave her the strength to preach at her son's funeral. She knew the only thing that could sustain her after such a devastating loss was the word of God which comforted her, so she began teaching the word of God to a group of older women.

In October 2012, the Lord called her to start a Prayer and Bible study Ministry called "The Fountain of Living Waters Ministry". It is a Teleconference Ministry whose sole purpose is how to make Heaven. After teaching in the Ministry for 7 years, the Lord laid it on her heart to write this book "Preparation for our Journey to Heaven". This book provides a great guide to living the life Christ requires of His followers, so that we at the end can proclaim that we fought the good fight, finished the race, kept the faith and earned our citizenship in Heaven.

Rose Mbamali lost her husband of fifty two years on May 31st, 2016, with whom she had 5 wonderful children, 18 lovely grandchildren and one energetic great grandson. She currently lives in Suffolk, Virginia , USA.